W9-ARG-565

Economic Justice

An Evangelical Perspective

By Richard J. Niebanck

CHRISTIAN SOCIAL RESPONSIBILITY SERIES

Division for Mission in North America
Lutheran Church in America

The *Christian Social Responsibility Series* is a publication of the
Division for Mission in North America, Lutheran Church in America.
The *Series,* along with other DMNA printed and audiovisual
materials, is produced through the Interpretation Staff of the division.

John A. Evenson, Director of Interpretation
Fern Lee Hagedorn, Assistant Director
Anne Ellis, Researcher-Writer
Michael Young, Designer
Brad Hess, Cover Photo

Library of Congress Cataloging in Publication Data

Niebanck, Richard J.
  Economic justice.

  Bibliography: p.
  1. Christianity and economics.
  2. Christianity and justice. I. Title.
  BR115.E3N46   261.8'5   80-27673
  ISBN 0-93536-03-9

Printed in USA

2

CONTENTS

Preface

This book was written for two specific purposes: to provide background for the delegates to the Tenth Biennial (1980) Convention of the Lutheran Church in America as they considered a proposed statement on economic justice, and to assist the leadership of the church in the interpretation of economic issues from an evangelical perspective. The first purpose was accomplished when on June 30, 1980, the convention adopted the social statement "Economic Justice: Stewardship of Creation in Human Community" (See Appendix A).

The mandate for a major social statement on economic justice was given by the Ninth Biennial Convention of the church in a resolution calling for "an intensive study of international economic relations and . . . the consideration of a major policy statement on that subject in 1980."[1] That resolution, intended to implement one dimension of the statement "Human Rights: Doing Justice in God's World," which was adopted by the same convention, recognized the great disparity between the affluent minority and the impoverished majority in the world community, and the deprivation of the latter "of such basic human rights as those of nutrition, housing, work and fair compensation for work and/or resources."

The wording of the resolution echoes the concerns about world hunger expressed by yet another convention, the Seventh, in 1974. That convention recognized the necessity both for an immediate response by the church to starvation of epidemic proportions as well as a long-term response to endemic poverty in both the developed and the developing countries. In its actions authorizing a special appeal for funds, the convention directed that "a portion of the collected funds be used to express the concern of this church to government agencies and representatives,"[2] and that the church join with other organizations "to advocate changes in governmental practices and processes which inhibit or prevent [food and development] aid from reaching those parts of the world's population suffering from severe hunger."[3]

The political dimension of the problem was delineated in the statement "Toward the Development of a United States Food Policy," issued by Lutheran World Relief (LWR) and endorsed by the convention "as a position of this church in representation to the Canadian and United States governments and other national and international organizations"[4] (See Appendix B). In its endorsing action the convention acknowledged:

1. That the urgent problems of hunger and malnutrition are inexorably woven into a broader perspective which includes issues of population growth, economic and industrial development, and environmental deterioration;

2. That concerns for social justice and human dignity must be reflected in our response to such global crises; and

6

3. That world hunger cannot be satisfied by charitable gifts or by governments alone.[5]

Finally, the concern was reflected in a four-part resolution authorizing the church to institute a World Hunger Appeal in which gifts were to be used in the following ways:

1. Immediate relief of world hunger;
2. Development of programs to deal with endemic need;
3. Sensitizing of the constituency of the church to the nature and extent of the crisis; and
4. A critical address to governmental programs designed to deal with this crisis.[6]

The social statement on economic justice and this background book may be seen as a result of the church's experience in carrying out the World Hunger mandate. It is intended as a response to the need for a basic theological-ethical framework within which to address a host of complex issues. The Division for Mission in North America, in developing a statement on economic justice, has attempted not so much to give answers to problems as to provide a theological tool for asking the right questions.

These documents represent a long and painstaking process of consultation throughout the church; the preparation and review of two major drafts and several revisions; and considerable research into current economic, theological and ethical literature. The drafters have benefited from the advice of countless persons of expertise, and of many more who have shared their experience as participants in the economy. The latter are primarily lay persons in the parishes of the church.

In view of the complexities of the issue and the need for a sound theological foundation, the statement has been so developed as to provide a framework to undergird reflection and action that is theologically consistent, ecclesiastically responsible and politically effective. Rather than undertaking to describe or prescribe, the statement enunciates principles which will guide the community of faith as it responds to the issues in a variety of ways. The background book suggests some ways in which these normative principles may be applied in practical situations. While it follows the general progression of the statement, the book is not intended as an "official interpretation." On the contrary, it is but one of many tools to be employed by thoughtful and responsible interpreters as they "unpack" the issues to which the statement is addressed.

It should be noted that several earlier statements of the Lutheran Church in America speak directly to matters of economic justice:

1. "Race Relations" (1964) on equal economic opportunity and the church's selective use of its power as employer and purchaser of goods and services in the interest of racial justice

2. "Poverty" (1966) on full employment or guaranteed income for persons unemployed as a result of counter-inflationary policy

3. "World Community" (1970) on development aid—especially through multilateral channels—to poor countries and the responsible management and just sharing of the resources of the seas

4. "The Human Crisis in Ecology" (1972) emphasizing the responsible and just stewardship of the world's finite resources

5. "Human Rights" (1978) including basic economic rights, participation in and co-determination of decisions regarding the conditions of life and work, and understanding of private property in terms of responsible stewardship

6. "Aging and the Older Adult" (1978) including public policy goals to guarantee secure and dignified life to elderly persons[7]

The present statement should therefore be read in light of these earlier ones, and the role of government set forth here should be understood in light of the statement "Church and State: A Lutheran Perspective" (1966) and the background booklet by the same name.[8]

The views expressed in the present book are those of its author and are in no sense to be construed as an official judgment on the part of either the Lutheran Church in America or its Division for Mission in North America. They are offered as aids to the church and its members as they confront the many and complex issues that must be dealt with as part of a creative search for economic justice.

The author acknowledges with gratitude the many useful insights contributed to him by a host of persons both within and outside the constituency of the church. Deserving of special mention are his colleagues in the Department for Church in Society, William H. Lazareth, George H. Brand and Bruce D. Marshall. Finally, he expresses thanks to Anne Ellis whose skillful editing significantly reduced the "fog index" of the book; to Estelle Hyder for her painstaking secretarial assistance; and to Florence Tolbert and Dorothy Oscar who produced the final manuscript.

Richard J. Niebanck
Division for Mission in North America

Introduction

It is not easy to develop church policy on ethical issues of public concern. And among such issues, economic justice poses some particularly bewildering problems. Part of the difficulty lies in the enormous range and complexity of questions that relate to economics and justice. More basic, however, is the fact that economic activity lies at the very core of our personal lives. Grounded in the reproduction of the concrete stuff of human life, and involving the management and distribution of wealth, economic activity is as basic as sexuality to our existence in this finite material world. Along with politics, love and faith, economic concerns have an intimacy shared by few other issues.

Economics as an intellectual discipline has long sought to achieve a scientific rigor comparable to that of the physical sciences. Present-day economics claims to be *de*scriptive rather than *pre*scriptive, and exalts such virtues as rationality and objectivity. Yet scholarly discussions of economic matters usually turn into impassioned exchanges revealing clear value-preferences in which one person's fact is another one's bias. In a moment of disarming candor, one economist has spoken of his own "irrational passion for dispassionate rationality."[1]

This is hardly surprising. What appears to be rational analysis frequently conceals the arbitrary, the whimsical and the self-serving which may be subject to effective challenge by other interpretations and presuppositions. Economic analysis is particularly vulnerable to such attack, for when our security, comforts and pleasures are at stake, the temptation to rationalize is very great indeed.

Lying as they do at the heart of human experience, economic activity and discourse deal with the fundamental feature of human life that also engages the discipline of ethics: human social relations. The two economically rooted commandments admonishing us not to steal or covet are neighbor-related. And, as Luther makes clear in both the Small and Large Catechisms, these commandments imply that we are obliged to render such help and service as will increase our neighbor's economic welfare and general happiness. In this the church parts company with contemporary economic thought and links the discipline of economics with the ethical concept of justice.

Because of this crucial joining of ethics and economics the church must concern itself with all aspects of economic life. The material gifts of God, including the human capacity for work, frequently become barriers to the achievement of real community and, indeed, objects of false worship and devotion. For this reason the church is obliged to speak on economic issues both pastorally to its people and prophetically to the world.

The following discussion is based on a number of assumptions that will be developed in due course:

1. God the Creator calls all persons to exercise a steward-

ship of resources, work and wealth for their neighbors' sake.

2. Justice is the social form of God's creating and preserving love in a world that is both finite and sinful.

3. God's love, in the form of justice, is mediated through institutions and laws, as well as through persons and groups acting and interacting out of motives of self-interest.

4. Justice is not inferior to love, but an extension of it.

5. Conscious Christian action for justice is an expression of the love of Christ working through the believer for the sake of many neighbors.

6. The incarnate Son of God through his death and resurrection frees and empowers his Body, the church, to engage in the struggle for justice within the material world.

7. The Spirit both inspires and corrects the church's vision of what is required by justice within a given set of historical and social circumstances.

8. An authentically Christian approach to economic issues begins with a lively doctrine of stewardship.

All of the foregoing assumptions are based on the evangelical view that love of neighbor—whether in the form of individual kindness or social justice—is both the grateful response of the faithful to the saving initiative of God in Christ and the means by which God extends love to the people whom he created and for whom Christ died. The neighbor is thus seen as the *end and object* of divine love and not the means through which the believer seeks and loves God.

Throughout this book the term "evangelical" is used to signify the Christ-centered faith that was recovered and proclaimed by the Lutheran reformers. Such faith lies within the classical Christian tradition set forth in Holy Scripture and the three ecumenical creeds: the Apostles', the Nicene and the Athanasian. As such, it is to be distinguished from the biblical literalism that today calls itself "evangelical."

The plan of this book is as follows. The first two chapters sketch a picture of the economic world today. They seek to identify some of the major questions under current debate, and consider the remarriage of economic with political and ethical discourse. The third chapter offers a critique of moralistic approaches to economic questions, while the fourth analyzes the misinterpretation of Scripture to support moralism. Chapter five sets forth the elements of an evangelical approach to the issues, and chapter six concludes with suggestions concerning the role of the church in the struggle for economic justice.

This book is only a beginning. It invites people who have experienced the liberating power of Christ in their lives to engage in that stewardship of meanings and values which is uniquely theirs.

CHAPTER 1

The Political Dimension

Economic questions generally hold little interest for most people unless their own well-being is directly at stake. Fiscal and monetary policy, the balance of payments, international trade and development suggest to most of us an arcane science whose myriad complexities render it altogether forbidding. Even when inflation, industrial flight or other economic developments threaten our material security, we feel baffled and angry but have little to guide us in our efforts to understand what is happening and what can be done about it. As a rule we prefer to leave economics to the experts.

Separate Spheres

Many people tend to think of economics and politics as two separate realms. Government action in the economic sphere is considered extraordinary if not suspect. And economic choice is thought to be a private individual transaction in the market place. Politics, it is felt, should stay clear of economics.

This is not to contend, of course, that Americans and Canadians have been totally unaware of the link between politics and economics. For many years organized labor, for example, has demonstrated how political power can be used effectively to obtain desired legislation on such bread-and-butter issues as the minimum wage, collective bargaining rights and on-the-job safety. Wage controls have been resisted by labor, and price controls by industry. Fiscal and monetary policy and their impact upon unemployment and inflation continue to engage the lobbyists of both business and labor.

The relationship between unemployment and inflation and the matter of effective economic controls have gradually become topics of conversation beyond the bounds of academia, but they continue to be too abstract to engage the interest of most people. The current term "stagflation"—economic stagnation coupled with inflation—suggests that former theory no longer applies: unemployment and inflation no longer appear to operate in an inverse relationship to each other. Yet politicians continue to prescribe the old medicine: increased spending and plentiful money for unemployment; "the balanced budget" (more sacred icon than reality) and tight money for inflation. Meanwhile the public retreats in confusion to less troubling subjects.

So it is that unless their immediate situations are affected most people are content to leave economics to the economists. Although their particular interests as workers, business persons or retirees may occasionally require political involvement, the economic big picture remains obscure.

There are at least two reasons for this. One is a sense of the overwhelming size of the major economic actors—big business, big labor, big government—and a consequent sense of insignificance, even helplessness, in the face of such power. The other is the notion that economics is a precise science operating according to its own inherent principles—principles that are comprehensible only to the experts. This assumption, which will be explored in the next chapter, can be traced to the eighteenth century when the world was viewed in mechanistic terms.

The prevailing rationalism of that time was less interested in questions of right and wrong ("Whatever is, is right," said Alexander Pope) than it was in discovering what made the world "tick" (to use the prevailing Deist metaphor of the universe as a watch wound by the divine Watchmaker). In such a context economics was seen as the proper domain of the technician, not the moralist. An economic "good" might well be a moral "bad" without in any way interfering with the proper functioning of the economic mechanism.

The ticking watches or spinning tops to which the universe and its component parts were likened in the eighteenth century have now yielded to such other models and metaphors as the system of interrelated equations set forth by the neoclassical economists, the energy conversion system or the cybernated machine. Yet the idea of the economy as a mechanism persists. "How does it work?" and "How can it be fixed?" still assumes greater importance in current economic thinking than "For whom should it be constructed and made to work?"

The Energy Crisis

It may well be that what is generally referred to as the energy crisis will soon change the general aversion to economic discourse. Not that it will turn many of us into economic pundits. Rather, it will force us to realize that the fundamental economic issues are neither remote nor abstract. We will learn that economics is very close to politics, that "what is" is the result of political choice and the exercise of political power in specific ways. Increasingly and in greater numbers we will begin to ask why such political and economic choice cannot, at least in part, be our own.

The energy crisis has put economic issues at center stage of the popular consciousness and called into question the notion that the economy operates like a machine. People will not long continue to regard the economy as they would a household appliance: conscious of it only when it breaks down, then searching frantically for a specialist to make repairs. Not only will economic questions occupy more of our waking moments, but they will increasingly be seen as *political* in their implications, requiring fundamental shifts in the realms of power and of values, rather than the tinkering of economic technicians.

The reasons for this shift are not difficult to find. The current energy crisis was touched off in 1973, not by some malfunction in the global economic machine, but by the deliberate choice of the Arab members of OPEC (Organization of Petroleum Exporting Countries) to embargo oil shipments to the United States and the Netherlands. Suddenly the mechanism of the economy yielded to the game of politics. Oil—a vital economic resource—became a political weapon in the struggle between Israel and the Arab world. And, just as suddenly, powerful industrial economies were revealed as utterly dependent upon those who controlled the sources of crude oil. Economists, accustomed to making predictions within an orderly framework of recognized assumptions, were suddenly confronted with a totally new situation in which all bets were off.

Since the awakening of the industrial societies to the unpleasant realities unleashed by the 1973 OPEC embargo, reflection about economics in political terms has grown apace. The initially overwhelming problem of oil as a weapon in a particular quarrel has been replaced by more fundamental and long-term questions. Who is to control the sources of supply, the refining, pricing and distribution of oil? Who determines, and by what criteria, when and where new fields will be developed? How and when should a shift be made to what alternate sources of energy? These and related questions—involving as they do the distribution and realignment of political and economic power both within and among nations—will not be solved by the orderly operation of economic laws or by a non-existent free market.

A New Politics

The politics of energy is in many ways a radically new politics. The determination of "who gets what, when and where" is increasingly being made by a new set of political actors. National governments and conventional political procedures are showing themselves unequal to the challenge of developing coherent energy policies and of regulating the energy business. The global politics of petroleum appears beyond the effective reach of national governments. It is, of course, true that governments can cause episodic disruptions in the activity of transnational business by holding hostage a vital commodity, as in the 1973 boycott; or by withholding technology vital to developing the resources of another country, as in the U.S. ban on the export of high technology to the Soviet Union to protest the occupation of Afghanistan.[1] It is also true that politicians frequently attack the public image of particular corporations through "scapegoating" as exemplified by congressional threats to break up or otherwise penalize the oil companies.

It is clear that such disruptive tactics will occur from time to time in the future. And it is possible that the competition for oil may figure prominently in an East-West confrontation. In the long run, however, conventional politics within and among nations may well decline in importance in the face of an increasingly integrated world political economy. The transnational corporations with vast resources of technology and information will pose a growing challenge to the supremacy of national law and military might.

The limits of effective state action are already evident. It is the energy companies that decide when and where new oil fields shall be developed—decisions with far-reaching political consequences. Recently the World Bank considered the financing of new oil field development in the Third World. One of the transnational oil companies lobbied successfully against the program, arguing that such financing should be left to the private sector, thereby keeping the political determination of "where," "when" and "how much" in the hands of the multinationals.[2]

Not only does the perpetuation of such control guarantee restriction of production in order to keep prices high; it materially affects the political and economic future of countries with oil reserves which the multinationals choose not to develop. Indeed, political judgments as much as geological and other technical considerations seem to figure in the choice of fields for new development. Some countries, believed to have resources of their own, may continue indefinitely to be oil-dependent because of oil industry decisions.

For these reasons it is conceivable that the age of a petroleum-based world economy may end well before the depletion of world oil reserves. Transnational corporations will figure prominently in decisions concerning a shift of energy sources and the nature of such sources. The oil companies are acquiring extensive holdings in gas, coal and uranium, and therefore the power to be among the world's chief energy planners. Since they combine disproportionately large amounts of information about potential energy sources with the flexibility of central decision-making, these companies will be able to determine the distribution of work and wealth, as well as the quality of life of millions of persons throughout the world.

Conservation and Productivity

The energy crisis has served to focus attention on the profligate consumption patterns of industrialized societies. It has made us aware of the threat posed by such unbridled consumption in terms of the ultimate exhaustion of nonrenewable resources as well as environmental contamination in such forms as "greenhouse effect," water pollution or atomic radiation. We have been confronted with the lopsided ratio of consumption between the industrialized countries and the Third World.

Oil consumption is a dramatic index of this imbalance. In 1976 the United States, with six percent of the world's population, used 29 percent of all petroleum consumed. Despite Third World efforts to industrialize, particularly in the so-called middle income countries, their petroleum use was miniscule. China, for example, increased its consumption by 30 percent between 1975 and 1976. Even so, with one quarter of the world's population, China was responsible for only 2¼ percent of the world-wide oil consumption during that period.[3]

All this suggests that the concern about conservation generated in response to the energy shortage may be a luxury that only the wealthy can afford. In the case of oil, development of new sources is almost entirely in the hands of corporate entities whose accountability is to their shareholders. With no world agency to plan or govern the exploitation of resources for the benefit of all, and especially the poorest, the private sector will make crucial decisions on far narrower grounds. The results will not be dictated by free competition or even by such factors as relative accessibility. They will be planned and projected in the interest of the corporations as perceived by them. The prospects for the less developed countries (LDCs) to proceed with industrialization will depend in large part upon the political acceptability of these countries to the transnational corporations.

The suggestion that concern about conservation is a luxury of the rich also applies domestically within the industrialized countries. Economic slowdown with inflation and unemployment brought on by the energy crisis takes its heaviest toll on the poor. It is comparatively easy for the affluent leadership of a country to enjoin belt-tightening when the leadership itself will continue to live in relative security. However, for the working poor, the elderly, persons of minority status or the unemployed young the situation is quite different. The fate of these people, though they may indeed be relatively well off by world standards, will, like the fate of the poor everywhere, be increasingly determined by central decisions in which they were not permitted to share.

Emerging Issues

The energy crisis is functioning as a stern pedagogue, radically reordering people's perceptions of economic reality. The economy can no longer be viewed as a machine which, once set in motion, is best left alone. It must be understood as the result of deliberate choices made by powerful actors. This shift in our understanding of basic economic realities is accompanied by a host of basic questions that will engage world society for the indefinite future. Among these questions are the following:

1. *Need versus appetite.* Have the Western nations become economies of gluttony? Have needs been so redefined that former luxuries have become necessities? If so, is the necessary restraint imposed by skyrocketing fuel prices perhaps a thing to be welcomed? In scaling

down their appetites, how can these economies avoid even greater unemployment? Will the alternative to leisured idleness with ample discretionary income be jobless idleness and the welfare client?

2. *Free markets/trade versus cartels.* Without a world government or transnational authority to protect the marketplace from manipulation how can dependent nations defend themselves against the strong-arm tactics of producer cartels? And if such tactics are permitted to some, why not to all?

3. *The environment.* This becomes crucial both in terms of oil dependency and the search for alternate energy sources. Several examples spring to mind: (a) contamination of the seas by oil spills and runaway wells; (b) serious talk of sacrificing recent gains in air quality in order to use coal; and (c) the inherent dangers of thermal pollution and radioactivity as inevitable by-products of nuclear power.

4. *The power of government.* The energy crisis has exposed the impotence of government in the face of both foreign producer cartels and domestic special interests. While it would seem that such fundamental economic decisions as those governing energy are the concern of all people, and therefore rightly belong to the political arena, there is a clear inability on the part of traditional politics to handle them. As we enter a period of slower economic growth, the conflict over scarce resources leads to a politics of distribution. What will be the agency to serve as arbiter among conflicting claims for finite benefits? The great debate of the 1980s may well be the shape of economic planning.

5. *Transnational corporate power.* The secrecy that often characterizes corporate management has created a growing popular paranoia toward the transnational corporations—those vast conglomerates formerly known as "multinationals." This is particularly true of the giant oil companies and the "politics of oil." How can these agents of transnational power be held accountable for their actions? The facility with which they are able to deploy resources, capital and skill renders them crucial agents in the distribution of work and wealth throughout the world community. Without transnational public authority can these actors be controlled? And if such a transnational regulatory authority were to be established could it be protected from domination by the very interests it would be expected to regulate?

6. *Ownership, property and justice.* Who "owns" a nonrenewable resource? The one who by accident of history happens to be sitting on it? Does the need for it constitute a moral claim on that resource? If so, what kind of institutional structures might be developed to translate such a claim into terms that are capable of adjudication? Who defines need, and how? Are the interests/needs of one-resource economies, e.g., some of the oil-producing countries, on a par with those of highly industrialized nations with petroleum-based economies? And what are the legitimate claims of developing countries in desperate need of oil-based fertilizers and fuel for farm implements?

While for the purposes of this discussion the issues have been set forth in terms of energy, they apply equally to a range of other economic necessities, e.g., technology. The point is that the energy crisis has suddenly made economics significant to ordinary people as never before. The separation of economic theory from moral and political issues is no longer to be taken for granted.

People whose concern for economic justice impels them into the arena of political activity will, in a very fundamental way, need to reorder and clarify their perceptions of economic life. Prerequisite to this task is a critical appraisal of competing ideological frameworks. It is to such an appraisal that we now turn.

CHAPTER 2

Economics and Ethics in a Changing World

The Legacy of Adam Smith

The birth of economics as a distinct sphere of human behavior and scientific inquiry is commonly held to be the publication in 1776 of Adam Smith's *The Wealth of Nations*. Imaginative and wide-ranging, Smith's mapping of economic terrain was a radical departure from earlier thought. Smith rejected the physiocrats' definition of farming as the only productive activity. He scorned the mercantilists' policy of state-nurtured and protected trade, and their equation of wealth with the accumulation of precious metals. The apostle of preindustrial capitalism, he proclaimed the division of labor, the circulation of commodities in a free market, wealth as the product of labor, and governmental non-interference in the economy.

Smith's work, like that of other epoch-making thinkers, contained the seeds of a controversy. Ebbing and flowing throughout succeeding centuries, it has now surfaced with great intensity: the relationship of economics on the one hand to ethics and politics on the other. Is economics an autonomous science governed by its own principles, or is it tied to and shaped by what are essentially moral and political considerations? Is economics an objective science or a moral art? Does it operate as a mechanism best left alone, or is it a dimension of politics? *The Wealth of Nations* implies a yes to both sides.

Smith's thought radiates a generous and optimistic spirit: a concern for human well-being coupled with the belief that individual pursuit of self-interest will achieve the good of all. It is self-interest, not benevolence, that secures one's material sustenance. Through the social division of labor and free exchange the needs of each and every person are satisfied. The diverse interests of the many are harmonized as if by an "invisible hand."

Justice, according to Smith, is essentially the non-interference of each member of society in the business of the other, with the assurance that contracts be legally enforced and collusion or monopoly prevented. Justice is thus both formal and primarily negative.

It can be seen at once that Smith combines elements of both the scientific "is" and the moral "ought." He makes a clean break with the Aristotelian/Thomistic view of justice: a giving to each what is one's due. And he parts company with the medieval canonists' preoccupation with the "just price." The price of a thing for Smith is regulated automatically by the operation of the market mechanism.

Smith's moral concern for human well-being is served by the unimpeded operation of an economy conceived in mechanistic terms. In his view, tampering with the economic mechanism in the name of morality can only wreak havoc and worsen the human condition. The operation of the "invisible hand" in regulating and harmonizing the irrational choices of individual persons is to be preferred to a deliberate attempt to arrange the economy according to rational morality.[1] Thus the founder of classical political economy sets the stage for the later ideological divorce of economics and ethics in the neoclassical school. The rich and expansive thought of Smith, while grounded in a positive view of human nature and the commitment to liberty as a preeminent principle of both politics and economics, also interprets the economy in mechanistic, objective and value-free terms.[2]

Smith's ideas may seem both refreshing and relevant to an observer of present-day economic chaos. It is seductive to contemplate simplicity and order when confronted with the apparent inability of contemporary ethicists, social planners and politicians to deal effectively with such persistent ills as the unemployment, urban decay and economic stagnation that plague all parts of the globe. And Smith's optimism provides an escape from the gloomy echoes of Ricardo in the current conflict between high technology and human labor, and of Malthus in the present-day specter of overpopulation and starvation. How much easier to leave, as did Smith, "the fortunes of those with whom we have no acquaintance" to the working of the "invisible hand."

However tempting the prospect of escape into a grand system that stands apart from political or moral restraints, there is no evading the reality of economics as ethical and political in its implications. Indeed, even if such a completely self-regulating system could be made to operate, the very decision to impose it upon society would be both moral and political in scope, reflecting both an idea of the moral "good" in the goals and functioning of the mechanism, and the political power to impose and enforce it.

That economics, ethics and politics are being push-pulled back together does not necessarily imply moral superiority of the present over the past. Nor does it commend the return to a precapitalist innocence that never, in fact, existed. Rather, this move toward reunion reflects a number of objective and clearly observable realities:

1. The articulation of economic demands by nations and societies newly possessed of the power to enforce them
2. The articulation of economic claims by the powerless with assurance of world-wide attention through the communications media, and eventual political impact
3. The complex and fragile webs of interdependence which render the world increasingly vulnerable to the decisions and actions of a few
4. A growing awareness of the limits of the world's natural resources, and the vulnerability of the biosphere

Economics and Freedom

The remarriage of economics and morality is evident even among those whose ideological preference is that of political libertarianism and liberal or free market capitalism. Once advocates of scientific objectivity in economics, they now assert individual liberty to be not merely the fundamental principle of the market mechanism, but a moral value as well. The free society is the good society. The truly free market—established and maintained through appropriate political decisions—assures the continuance of such a society.

They maintain, as did Smith, that deliberate economic intervention in the name of moral values such as justice is to subvert the economy and to thwart the very social well-being that is sought. Friedrich Hayek, one of the foremost exponents of this view, goes so far as to argue that economic justice is a concept devoid of substance.[3]

The evidence marshaled by these political and economic liberals to support their argument is formidable:

1. The manifest failure of politically motivated government programs specifically designed to deliver economic justice

2. The historic success of capitalistic societies in securing "the good life" or an ever-ascending standard of living

3. The penchant of countless people in both the socialist East and the capitalist West for underground or informal economic activity: uncontrolled, untaxed, cash only, and off-the-books

4. The inability of government to prevent illicit traffic in goods and services judged to be morally wrong or socially harmful

In its popular form this "possessive individualism" is put forth by such writers as Ayn Rand, for whom selfishness is a cardinal virtue. And the free market as the model of the good society is proclaimed in a popular idiom by economists Milton and Rose Friedman.[4] Rand and the Friedmans would agree with Smith that concern for those in misery is "nothing but . . . affected and sentimental sadness" which can only "render miserable the person who possesses it."[5]

In making their case, the protagonists of liberty and the free market at times aim their barbs at Christian ethicists and church leaders. Hayek, for example, charges that the idea of social justice has been taken over from the socialists by most teachers and preachers of morality to replace their lost faith in a supernatural revelation. He charges Christians with substituting "a temporal for a celestial promise of justice."[6]

The gross misreading of historic Christian teaching reflected in such statements is perhaps understandable, in view of the considerable degree to which the rationalism of the Enlightenment has been absorbed by popular religion in the West. What Hayek and others have totally overlooked, however, is the long tradition of social justice in Christian thought which antedates the emergence of the liberal ideology of possessive individualism.[7] In the light of that tradition the present-day concern of the church for social justice, far from being the substitution of a new faith for one that is old and outworn, is both a reaffirmation and a recovery of the understanding of co-humanity fundamental to Christianity. This concept, together with the realistic assessment of human nature as finite and sinful, contrasts markedly with the optimistic individualism advanced by Hayek, the Friedmans and Rand.

These apostles of economic liberty are also vulnerable to the empirical criticism that in countries where their ideology has been deliberately chosen to inform public policy the result has not been liberty but another kind of authoritarianism. The 1973 coup in Chile was engineered in part by transnational oligopoly capitalists in the name of free market capitalism. Furthermore, the economic policies proclaimed by the new regime, while based upon free market theory, have not brought an open society to the country. Likewise in the Philippines, democracy was suspended in order to save the private enterprise that allegedly creates democracy. South Korea, Taiwan, South Africa and Argentina present other examples of un-freedom in the so-called "free world."

Perhaps a more basic irony is that while the free market ideology renounces interventionist government policies, there is no lack of such intervention in countries which have adopted that economic framework. It is not that the regimes have abstained from intervention in the economy, but that their interventionist policies have been designed to favor industrial development, the growth of an export economy and an affluent urban sector.

As this discussion suggests, there lurks within the economic debate a fundamental, indeed theological, disagreement concerning the nature of humanity and the world. Such a disagreement affects both the various descriptions of economic reality and the prescriptions which are brought to it. In conflict with the proponents of a reborn economic liberalism are a host of otherwise disparate advocates whose call is for economic justice.

Economics and Justice

From the late eighteenth century on, "justice" and "economics" were thought to inhabit quite separate spheres. To be sure, laws enforced by governments were regarded as necessary for the protection of property rights and the enforcement of contracts, and economic disputes were adjudicated by the courts. But the concept of economic justice as the goal of economic activity, implying some sort of fair and equitable sharing of the economic product, quickly faded from Western economic theory and practice as the philosophical heritage of medieval Christendom retreated before the onrush of secularism.

But if justice and economics could not be successfully held together by the church, their rejoining began in the mid-nineteenth century through the movements of reform and revolution that accompanied the rise of industrial capitalism.

Foremost among the voices of radical criticism was that of Karl Marx. During the course of his lifetime Marx wove together the various strands of thought that became the basis for both an analytical critique of capitalism and a revolutionary program to overthrow it. Chief among these strands were utopian socialism, classical political economy, Hegelian dialectics and an essentially Hebraic understanding of human nature.

It is this variety within Marxist thought that renders it so fruitful as a tool of analysis and as a revolutionary ideology. While it is impossible to deal in any detail with Marxism and Marxist thought in the present discussion, its influence will be further noted in the two succeeding chapters.

How the ideas of Marx were employed as the official ideology of the Soviet state is an all too familiar story. The concept of the world-wide solidarity of workers yielded to a reborn Russian imperialism. Historical determinism was chosen rather than the humanism of the early Marx. A system of state capitalism was advanced under the socialist label, and the ideals of liberation and justice dissolved into Stalinist terror.

It was in response to this totalitarian and atheistic revision of Marxism that economic justice again became a theme in Western Christian thought. Signal examples of this were the encyclical *Rerum Novarum* of Pope Leo XIII (1891) and *Quadragesimo Anno* of Pope Pius XI (1931). The same themes were advanced in such later encyclicals as *Pacem in Terris* (1963) of Pope John XXIII, and the considerable body of Catholic thought on justice and development.

Feeling the pressure of Marxism within the laboring class, and fearful that the movement would win large numbers of the faithful, the Roman Catholic church looked into its own heritage—chiefly Thomas Aquinas' doctrine of natural law—for a concept of justice that would answer the needs of the poor and the working class. The result was the Leonine encyclical, the founding of Christian Democratic parties, the involvement of clergy in the settlement of labor disputes in the United States, and the growth of a Catholic Left. After World War II these developments led to even more radical expressions including the Worker Priest movement in France and, most recently, the "base communities" (local revolutionary self-help groups) and the theology of liberation in Latin America.

From Radicalism to Pragmatism: American Labor

The early years of the labor movement in America were marked by a ringing call for social and economic justice.

Such movements as the International Workers of the World (IWW) were noted for their social radicalism, which carried over into the industrial unions as opposed to the more conservative craft unions. At the present time the youthful United Farm Workers movement has espoused a radicalism similar to that which characterized union activity in earlier years.

The evolution of American labor is a good example of the move from radicalism to pragmatism. This is, in part, evidence of the flexibility and adaptability of Western capitalism which at various stages accommodated the demands of labor and made possible a "buying in" on the part of the labor movement. Industrial conflict became managed conflict; radical opposition from without became loyal opposition from within. Proposals which had at first seemed utopian were eventually enacted. The 1932 platform of the American Socialist Party, for example, is now law. Such accommodation is best characterized in the advice attributed to Bismarck: We must change in order to remain the same.

The world is now faced with a vast wave of hitherto silent "outsiders" who alternately demand admittance to the emerging global community of work and wealth, and call for a radical transformation of prevailing economic and political arrangements. Their voices are heard in the clash of two contrasting ideas of justice.

Commutative and Distributive Justice

Members of any club generally deal with each other as equals in terms of pragmatic reciprocity. Justice or fairness is understood to be the give and take among equals in the context of an agreed-upon code of self-restraint which is to everyone's benefit. But when the outsider clamors to get into the club, the rhetoric used is of the unjustly excluded, the one who needs a foothold from which to participate.

The excluded one clamors to get in for a number of reasons: because the club is gobbling up a disproportionately large share of the common resources; because it exploits the excluded one's cheap labor and resources without giving fair return or even a vote; because the club controls most of the skills and technology which would, if shared, make possible something better than subsistence living for the world's majority. The outsider struggles for inclusion on moral grounds. Once inside, pragmatic bargaining replaces moral struggle.

The club members deal with one another as equals in terms of what Aristotle calls *commutative justice*. The outsider demands the means to participate in terms of Aristotle's *distributive justice*. The outsider says, in effect: "I, as a human being, have a right to be included because by my continued exclusion I am the more impoverished and robbed of my dignity. And you, the privileged, have the obligation under justice to open the door and supply me with what I need in order to participate. *Simply to declare the door to be open without providing me with the means to enter is to program my certain failure and to rob me of yet more of my dignity as a human being.*"

This is essentially the argument supporting the establishment of what is now generally called a New International Economic Order (NIEO).[8] This terminology was established by the so-called "Group of 77," a coalition of developing countries, and gained prominence in a special session of the United Nations General Assembly in 1975. Such a "new order" would include an increased sharing of technology with the less developed countries, better terms of trade between the less developed and developed countries, and more generous assistance programs, preferably under multilateral auspices.

Though they seem to exist in sharp contrast to each other, the communities of poverty and affluence are in fact closely tied together. The industrially developed sector of the world depends upon many of the poor countries for cheap raw materials and primary products with which to supply its industries and satisfy the demands of seemingly insatiable consumer economies. The poor countries, in turn, depend upon the wealthy for finished products and capital goods which they purchase at ever increasing prices, incurring constantly greater debt.

The less developed countries (LDCs) have long maintained that the members of GATT (General Agreements on Trade and Tariff)—characterized as a wealthy nations' trading association—have simply declared the door to be open without doing anything significant to correct unequal terms of trade or to encourage domestic manufacturing through inexpensive financing and transfers of technology. They feel that the industrialized nations should stop pretending to a non-existent mutuality among equals and begin to help establish a true equality through distributive justice. Unless there are qualitatively significant moves in this direction, the long-term projections for the less developed countries are poor. Unless the volume and direction of international capital and development aid are dramatically altered the gap between the developed and the less developed countries will continue to grow wider.

Although the less developed countries contain over 60 percent of the world's total population, they produce and consume only 15 percent of the global output of goods and services. According to official UN statistics, in 1970 the average per capita income in the LDCs amounted to only one-twelfth of the average per capita income of the developed industrialized countries. The UN study concludes that if the structures and institutional relationships now governing world-wide economic growth continue to operate in the same way, that ratio might fall to one-eighteenth by the year 2000. That is a prescription for intense social upheaval and political violence. It is in this context that the concept of distributive justice is, after so long a time, beginning to gain currency.

The Analytical Debate

The world-wide struggle sketched above is accompanied by an intense theoretical debate about which picture of the world is correct, what factors are causative, and how change may be effected. This debate reflects the inevitable connection between what is said about reality and the observer's standpoint within that reality. It is doubly appropriate in view of the sometimes devastating attacks that the various observers make on each others' claims to objectivity.

The economic debate today ranges from the technical to the unabashedly political. At the technical end of the continuum are questions which presuppose the existence of a functioning economic system. The questions ask not whether the system is morally good or evil, but rather how it works and how it is evolving. The technical questions about "stagflation" are an example: (1) Has the hitherto assumed inverse relationship between inflation and unemployment actually changed, or is it a matter of the long versus the short run? (2) If the relationship has indeed changed, what systemic evolution does that change imply? (3) What new interventionist strategies, if any, must now be devised to answer the new situation if, indeed, one exists?

It is important to use the term "technical" in a qualified sense for, depending on where one stands within the economic system, the same issue may be seen as either technical or moral and political. This is true especially in the case of those adversely affected, e.g., the unemployed. What may be "merely technical" to one group may be a highly charged political issue to another. Of the two economic extremes posed by stagflation, inflation is the greater burden for the middle classes: professionals, business executives and civil servants—to say nothing of the elderly and disabled who must live on fixed incomes. Unemployment, on the other hand, poses the greater threat to workers, blacks and ethnic minorities, since they are generally the ones first affected by efforts to reach "natural" levels of employment in the name of driving down inflation. Though stated in terms of economic principles, such decisions are inevitably laden with political implications.

The tension between the technical and the political is also evident in international economics. How, for example, one analyzes underdevelopment and dependency is for the poor anything but a purely technical matter. The following example serves to illustrate the point:

In certain island dependencies of the United States land lies fallow while the local inhabitants pay exorbitant prices for foodstuffs imported from the mainland. Tourists may purchase alcoholic beverages and luxury goods at cheap prices, yet the poor people of the countryside cannot get inexpensive food. Furthermore, the lack of cheap public transportation makes it practically impossible for the poor to avail themselves of the relatively lower prices in the supermarket, while the wealthy have easy access by automobile.

This situation is by no means unique, though details may vary. In many non-industrial countries land is underutilized or lies fallow, the property of a hereditary aristocratic class. Or it is used to produce cash crops for export to industrialized countries for conversion into processed foods, as is the case with sugar from the Dominican Republic; or to provide feed for meat production, such as feed grain from Haiti and Central America. Meanwhile, the local food economy does not provide reasonably priced nutrition for the local poor.[9]

The Dependency Debate

Situations such as the ones described above are the focus of heated analytical controversy. What is the relationship between affluence and poverty, superabundance and abject need? Must affluence depend upon poverty for its own continuation and growth? Is poverty a *necessary part* of capitalism and a *condition* of its existence? Or is it a temporary state, the result of such disparate factors as climate, natural resources, cultural "lag," or an insufficient rate of productive expansion?

Is poverty most effectively confronted through objective methods of diagnosis and treatment (fact finding and problem solving) or through moral criticism and political action (fault finding and revolution)? It is in terms of such questions that nations and the emerging world society are debating the issues of economic justice.

The response to these questions reveals the polarization of the ideological and political Left and Right. The Left has espoused the dependency theory which seeks to prove empirically that capitalism, whether national or transnational, in fact *needs* poverty in order to survive, and that capitalist growth both produces and is predicated on the growth of poverty or the development of underdevelopment.

The ideological Right dismisses the dependency theory as a faulty analysis of the relationship between rich and poor societies on a national and world scale. It sees poverty as a temporary problem which can be solved through technological know-how and increased growth. Poverty is seen as an essentially parasitic phenomenon which feeds on capitalism and is perpetuated by poorly conceived welfare programs and other public policies that discourage initiative, productivity, investment and growth.

Right-wing ideologues fluctuate between a "can do" optimism about the possibility of solving the so-called poverty problem, and a judgmental condemnation of the poor themselves. They also contend that although dependency relationships may indeed exist in certain instances, it cannot be demonstrated that poverty is always and everywhere tied to affluence. Such accidental factors as a lack of natural resources or an inhospitable climate must also be considered.

Members of each ideological camp regularly accuse their opponents of being unscientific and class or culture bound, while protesting their own objective and scientific grasp of reality. The scientific socialism of the Left rails against so-called bourgeois sociology as an aspect of the false consciousness endemic to capitalism. Scholars with a capitalist orientation, meanwhile, accuse the Left of imposing on empirical reality a set of alien categories which distort rather than clarify.

Over the past decade and a half, various attempts have been made to transcend cultural and political particularity and achieve a theory of development that is generally applicable.[10] These efforts have not fared well, however, and have been attacked for harboring hidden cultural and political biases. Critics have contended that such approaches nearly always imply that development is a replication—albeit in a shorter time frame—of the stages of Western social and political development, with the ultimate goal of pluralistic liberal democracy. In recent years the quest for such "value free" theory has abated in the face of criticism, but it has by no means disappeared.[11]

Current—Crosscurrent

While earlier theoreticians saw economics as a discipline unrelated to public decision making, today's thinkers are much less certain. Neoclassicists, as already noted, object to a massive government presence in economic affairs, and wish to restore the free market as the chief regulator of the economy. Their view would restore the purity of an economic model which operates by its own principles, free from intervening manipulation and the imposition of extraneous value biases.

Yet, their public advocacy is unabashedly political and moral in content, as witness the recent popular writings and the television series of Milton and Rose Friedman. Their rhetoric is not without its own version of what constitutes "proper" government intervention. And in the case of business leaders, behavior and rhetoric do not necessarily coincide.

By way of contrast, other advocates, declaring that economics should properly be concerned with the quality of life, seek for avenues leading to such goals as greater distributive justice and ecological preservation. Among these persons some outline their programs in Marxian terms. Others draw on Aristotelian/Thomist natural law which informed the economic discourse of medieval canonists before the Enlightenment and the industrial revolution. Still others combine elements of both Marx and Aristotle.

Then there is that amorphous assembly of those who, whatever their ideological tinge, are to a greater or lesser degree opposed to high technology. In its more extreme manifestations this position is technophobic and, like the temperance movement of an earlier day, in favor of "total abstinence" from high energy technology, especially nuclear power.

In its more moderate form (appropriate technology) this orientation questions the long-range implications of increased dependency upon centrally produced energy. It suggests that the energy repertoire should include the development of decentralized energy sources which render the community less dependent and therefore less vulnerable, and reinforce or revive local self-reliance. The following checklist would lend itself to other technology choices as well: (1) decentralized energy sources; (2) low capital investment; (3) user management; (4) conservation of nonrenewable resources; and (5) environmentally harmonious installations.

The Technocratic Mind

Looming above all of these disparate pictures of the economic world, one has established itself nearly everywhere, transcending seemingly incompatible cultural traditions and political ideologies. This is the technocratic model. Regarding the world as a spaceship, guided and controlled by increasingly sophisticated information systems, the technocratic worldview is aptly named "cybernetic." Reality is perceived as a set of systems: the answer to disorder is the use of increasingly effective control mechanisms.

In contrast to the neoclassical economist who sees the market mechanism as processing the aggregate choices of individuals, the technocrat approaches the world as an organism with various systems that must operate harmoniously and receive the necessary maintenance, i.e., information (nervous system); life sustenance (circulatory system); infrastructure (skeleton). And if the neoclassicist excludes questions of value from the functioning of the free market—whether posed theoretically by the ethicist or in practical terms by the politician—the technocrat conversely seeks to transform value questions into functional terms. Once goals and procedures have been established, information is translated into decisions under fixed operational norms, and directed toward fixed goals.

As crosscurrents in the life of this age, none of the ideological positions here described can be isolated or ascribed exclusively to one party, movement or social system. The technocratic mentality is found in capitalist countries as well as in those which espouse a Marxist-Leninist ideology. The proponents of "small is beautiful" may be coupon clippers enjoying the fruits of a high technology growth economy while experimenting with windmills and solar energy in protected bucolic settings. And the advocates of the untrammeled free market may be tenured professors whose endowed chairs assure them long-term security from the vagaries of the free market of ideas.

The contradiction between ideological commitment and economic practice is illustrated in the following vignette: A prominent European businessman was recently invited by an American college to be one of several lecturers on the future of the free market. During the discussion period he was asked why, if he were committed to the free market, the speaker accepted a regular government subsidy for his newspaper. He responded that (1) his newspaper was devoted to the news, not gossip and advertising; (2) because of this it had a smaller circulation, accepting a "number two" position; (3) since it was "number two" it attracted less advertising revenue than "number one"; and (4) in view of the sacrifice of its competitive position in order to perform a public service, it deserved the government subsidy.

Such special pleading and acceptance of public benefits by free market advocates is not unusual, reflecting both the impracticality of being ideologically pure in a complex world, and the universal human tendency to adopt a double standard.

These various crosscurrents of concept, analogy, dogma and behavior all reflect a rapidly changing and deeply divided world. Each proposes an economic diagnosis, each a prescription, and each undoubtedly contains an element of truth.

Technocracy, for instance, responds to the need for rational management of resources. Its achievements are impressive both in its corporate and public manifestations. It is a worldview which informs the vision of transnationalism with its commitment to maximized comparative advantage through centralized decision making about the deployment of capital.

It is precisely in the shining promise of technocracy that peril may lurk. People at all levels of society, having tried everything else, weary of disorder, hungering for some kind of predictability, will be tempted to put all their eggs into one technocratic basket, permitting the gradual erosion of deeply held values as economic dilemmas are broken down into discrete problems to be solved by central decision.

Who Is Included

Critics of technocracy and transnational enterprise are wary of the claim that everyone benefits under centralized management of resources. They point out that in reality "everyone" has thus far tended to exclude the poorest in both the developing and the industrialized countries. The much-heralded declarations of world financial leaders and institutions on behalf of the destitute seem to have led to little basic change.

Meanwhile, transfers of capital by the transnational corporations (TNCs) benefit only tiny sectors of affluence in the LDCs. Capital outflow is hidden. The underdeveloped areas of these countries will remain so, while the cities will continue to be tied not to the hinterlands of their own countries but to the economies of the industrialized nations. Labor, meanwhile, tied to locale and without sufficient organization to match the TNCs, will become increasingly susceptible to the central decision makers who can readily relocate capital in order to achieve what they perceive to be the most advantageous mix of productive factors. The central orchestration of raw materials, technology and labor on one hand, and markets on the other, creates for many the specter of total dependency.

What is most worrisome about the technocratic ethos is that it may eventually lead to the total abstraction of human beings, to their final reduction as mere factors in problems that need to be solved. In its most extreme manifestation it could lead to the classification of entire populations as redundant and, therefore, expendable. To the well-intentioned and humane devotees of technocracy such a suggestion may seem outrageous, far-fetched or sensational. However, one need only remind oneself of the recent debate concerning "triage"[12] to recognize that the unthinkable has, indeed, been seriously considered.

One thinks of the masses of poor people in Asia, Africa and Latin America, possessed of neither land nor skills. Lucky ones may be employed as migrant workers in the mines of South Africa or the coffee fields of the Ivory Coast.[13] But their usefulness as workers is only a matter of the time it will take to develop machinery that works more cheaply. One thinks of those among the urban poor in North America who by virtue of their exclusion from the larger society have become idle, dependent and hostile. Too often victims of persistent racism, they are forced to view from the outside a culture based on high technology whose fruits they have been programmed to desire but are not permitted to share.

Theory and Power

These cross currents of ideology and perception represent the clash of interests and the struggle for power which with mounting intensity characterize a rapidly evolving global community. As already noted, the debate between the advocates of global *inter*dependence and national *in*dependence or self-reliance, reflects the conflict between the established industrialized nations and the transnational corporations based inside them, with the emerging nations of Asia, Africa and Latin America. The former group exalts the virtues of stability, planned growth and comparative advantage. The latter espouses the need for local self-sufficiency through a diverse economy functioning within an integrated nation, local investment, manufacturing and markets, and an infrastructure which ties together city and countryside.

The same conflict underlies the debate over world rule of law, especially laws governing economic relations. The less developed countries variously contend that existing legal norms are essentially the rules of a "rich men's club" in the making of which they had no part. By complying with these rules the poor countries often feel that they are undermining their chances for success.

Likewise, the debate between no growth and rapid growth economists, between the advocates of nuclear power and nonproliferation, between free trade and preferential treatment, generally corresponds to the struggle between the so-called developed and developing worlds. It comes as no surprise that within the world Christian community the National Council of the Churches of Christ in the U.S.A. has adopted a position favoring a moratorium on peaceful nuclear development, while the position of the World Council of Churches favors transfer of nuclear technology to the less developed states. The WCC's attempt to inform its declarations with the principles of justice, participation and sustainability represents an effort to formulate a concept of economic justice that both transcends and bridges the interests and claims of these two distinct sectors of global society.[14]

Christians and the church are caught between the love of Christ which propels them into a world of needy neighbors, and utter bafflement in the face of a maze of conflicting perceptions and analyses. Though the chapters that follow do not attempt to remove the discomfort of this situation, they may provide a few useful landmarks for faithful disciples who must, in any case, get on with their Lord's business.

CHAPTER 3

Moralism: An Appraisal

How can the Christian community respond to and be faithful within a world of vast complexity and rapid change? What effective power does that community have to maintain its identity within the dehumanizing culture of modernity? Can Christians redirect or even stave off the so-called progress of that culture?

Much has been written about the pervasive self-centered privatism characteristic of Western culture. Dubbed "the culture of narcissism" by Harvard sociologist Christopher Lasch, it is both created and reinforced by an economic system designed to generate and satisfy demand for the paraphernalia of self-actualization, from cosmetics to assertiveness training. Correspondingly large amounts of ink have been used to expose a tendency on the part of the churches, in a frantic effort to be competitive, to follow the fad. The results are all around us in a processed positive thinking that is merchandised like convenience food. A capital-and-energy-intensive industry seeks to market confidence in formulas for personal success wrapped in something vaguely Christian. A variant product is the old-fashioned message of other-worldly bliss, done up in the trappings of mass entertainment and transmitted "live by satellite."

It is perhaps safe to assume that the vast majority of those reading this book have rejected the cult of self-fulfillment as both blasphemous and in contradiction to an authentic understanding of faithful stewardship. Yet there remains the danger that in the name of rejecting certain fads other fads may be embraced, and that something more subtle but equally false may replace contemporary mass market religion, aptly referred to as the "happiness industry." That "something" to which the well-intentioned so easily fall prey is moralism.

Moralism: Basic Characteristics

Manifested in a variety of politically individualistic as well as collective forms, moralism embodies some or all of the following features:

1. A single-minded reliance on simple solutions

2. A confidence in the goodness of the actor and the rightness of the act

3. A link between self-improvement and social amelioration, the one serving the interests of the other

4. A penchant for single-cause analysis of complex problems; a compulsion to fix blame, to identify "devils"

5. A corresponding tendency to engage in "single-issue" political action

6. Ignorance of/indifference toward the realities of political power and the necessity for trade-off and compromise

7. A belief in the possibility of Utopia; a perception of the ideal not as a standard of evaluation in an imperfect world, but as an attainable goal

From a theological standpoint, moralism is deficient for a number of reasons: (a) it is works righteousness; (b) it is built on a false confidence in the goodness of the actor; and (c) it makes the neighbor into a means for loving God or achieving a good conscience. Rather than beginning with God and ending with neighbor, moralism begins with neighbor and ends with self. Essentially unfree, it is inevitably unrealistic, incapable of compromise, and enamored of simple but spurious prescriptions.

Social/Self Improvement

The contemporary author Joan Didion describes moralism as the attempt "to improve one's world and one's self simultaneously."[1] And, referring to the moralism that has run through American foreign policy, she points to the tendency of Americans to view "the underdeveloped world as a temporarily depressed area in need mainly of People to People programs."[2] Or, as portrayed in John Updike's *The Coup,* America is possessed of a naive faith in its own inherent benevolence—a benevolence that answers catastrophic starvation by sending a mountain of Korn Kurls, Total and other processed foods.[3]

Moralism is inevitably self-serving, frequently serving the interests of an entire class or social group as well. Reinhold Niebuhr's trenchant analysis of "the ethical attitudes of the privileged classes"[4] is of timeless relevance: People tend to justify their privileged position in terms of their own moral virtue, and claim as their right what, in fact, has come to them as unearned advantage. Confident in their own rectitude, they embody what Didion calls "the particular [middle class] vanity of perceiving social life as a problem to be solved by the good will of individuals."[5] Both Niebuhr and Didion see apolitical individualism as incapable of achieving anything but a reinforcement of the self-righteousness of the comfortable.

Moralistic individualism may currently be seen in expressions of ecological piety by middle class America. Focusing on numerous commendable activities like the recycling of containers, such concern usually lacks a political dimension. Because it lacks focus, the well-meant gesture becomes a substitute for the political will that is required to support fundamental changes in patterns of consumption. This attitude is exemplified by the car-pooling commuter who seems, by and large, disinclined to push for the public measures necessary to secure a return to mass transit.

A striking example of such moralistic vanity is a loudly-heralded program launched by one of the major human potential movements. The initiators of this project attempt to generate confidence that if enough individuals have the will, the problem of starvation can be solved. They neither analyze the political and economic factors underlying maldistribution and underproduction, nor do they propose any strategy for the effective translation of aggregate individual commitment into corporate political power. The aim is simply to establish by means of mass auto-suggestion the idea that world hunger *can* be eliminated. In the words of the program literature, the establishment of the idea ("creation of context") is done by a repetitive process of "communication and enrollment, communication and enrollment."[6] The program begins and ends with the good intentions of individual persons. As "an idea whose time has come," the elimination of world-wide hunger has drawn to the organization a host of single-minded devotees and vast contributions of money. A centralized leadership exercises total control over these funds. The project has run newspaper advertisements encouraging readers to contribute money to voluntary relief agencies. Thus far this appears to be the only concrete action taken by the organization; and that action is couched solely in terms of individual benevolence.

Observers who question such an exercise in wish-fulfillment should ponder the fact that in many ways this project parodies the kind of individualistic moralism that has long been a characteristic of middle class Protestantism. Indeed, it is the secular flowering of an attitude nurtured in the churches of North America and Europe: an attitude in which the world was perceived as a moral gymnasium where duty and virtue were to be exercised, and the goodness of the "Gentle Galilean" emulated.

Collective Moralism

A prominent example of collective moralism in North America today is that of the public relations sermonettes — transmitted by both the print and electronic media — through which industrial corporations extol their contribution to the common good and advocate public policies that would promote both social progress and profits. One energy company, for instance, strategically places its inspirational essays opposite the editorial pages of major newspapers where it presents reflective, almost metaphysical justification of its behavior and tremendous earnings. And another reminds us repeatedly on television: "We're working to keep your trust."

By way of contrast, the low-budget collective moralism of the churches, while of older vintage, is far less nuanced and sophisticated. But more to the point: Whereas the moralism of the corporation is an expression of vast power, the moralism of the churches is more often than not a public posturing unsupported by any significant clout. The chief manifestation of such collective moralism is the official pronouncement through which a church body or council of churches endeavors to speak out against some perceived social ill, and offers prescriptive guidance to society and its agencies of government.

Frequently such social pronouncements lack theological roots in the living tradition of the faith community. If there is a nod toward theology at all, it is all too often in terms of the currently chic with heavy borrowings from ideology, philosophy or psychology. Such borrowings frequently lead to glaring inconsistencies. One encounters public statements on individual morality (e.g., abortion or sexuality) that are couched in individualistic, libertarian or quasi-personalist terms, while statements on social issues are frequently argued with a considerable dependence on Marxist thought. Such documents have dubious credibility because they communicate neither the essence of the church's historic witness nor an appreciation of the complexities of the issues being addressed.

Two factors stand out in collective moralism: (1) a simplistic notion that the witness of faith can be readily translated into prescriptive guidance to society, and (2) a lack of attention to political realities which cannot be altered without the astute application of political power.

Collective moralism carries with it two distinct dangers. On the one hand, it renders the church vulnerable to the cynical manipulations of interest groups which mask their self-serving purposes behind moral cant. Indeed, a church which does not match its "dovelike innocence" with a good measure of "serpentine wisdom" can easily find itself taken in. A real estate owner may hide behind an ecological banner while resisting a needed hydroelectric facility, thus forcing on the utility a greater reliance upon coal and nuclear power. Similar ecological arguments can be used to prevent low-income workers from locating near a corporate headquarters that has fled to an affluent suburb.

Corporations may mask their complicity in the "gentrification" of decaying city neighborhoods behind a claim of altruistic concern for the urban poor. Public employees' unions, interested primarily in saving jobs, may engage in righteous opposition to the closing of under-utilized public facilities on the grounds that curtailment of services even to a non-existent clientele is unjust.

On the other hand, moralism renders the church susceptible to a quixotic tendency to tilt away at any issue presented to it, with the predictable result that its constituency, as well as the larger community, soon learns to ignore what is essentially a knee-jerk response.

While much of the churches' collective moralism is ignored there is one variety that has become dangerously effective: single issue politics. Focusing on one narrowly defined issue, such collective moralism in fact poisons the political process and at times renders impossible the qualified achievement of the goal being sought. Furthermore, the practice of single issue politics invites undesirable side effects. It was in this fashion that Prohibition created the conditions for the flowering of organized crime. Similarly, a large middle class anti-draft movement of the late 1960s helped to produce not peace, but the "Vietnamization" of the American war in Southeast Asia.

The partisans of both sides in the abortion controversy have likewise damaged the political process. "Right to life" political action helped to bring about the defeat of two outstanding champions of social justice in both domestic and foreign policy.* "Right to life" advocates and their opponents have been accused of jeopardizing legislation which, through provisions designed to help working women keep their jobs as well as be mothers, could have helped to reduce the incidence of abortions. By its uncompromising identification of morality and law, single issue politics throws sand into the gears of the political process, polarizes the society and dampens the possibility for positive change.

The Sectarian Alternative

The collective moralism of mainstream Protestantism breathes the "can do" optimism which has long been at the heart of the American cultural ethos. That spirit,

---

*Representative Donald Fraser of Minnesota and Senator Dick Clark of Iowa.

60

though severely tested throughout the last decade, has not disappeared. Indeed, it is alive and growing in various forms of fundamentalist sectarianism which have set aside their traditional quietism and adopted an activist stance on a number of public issues. Representing a political spectrum ranging from an unabashedly old-fashioned capitalism and patriotism to a radical rejection of technological society, the new sectarian activists share clearly identifiable characteristics:

1. Use of the Bible as source book for unambiguous, ready-to-apply prescriptions for every dimension of life: "The Bible says it; I believe it; that settles it."[7]

2. Identification of Christianity with a moral code or lifestyle, whether in terms of rugged individualism or anti-technological communalism

3. A hostility toward certain social systems perceived as arrangements of "the devil," and commitment to reactionary, radical or populist programs designed to correct them

Thus the disappointed optimism of liberal Protestantism is being replaced by expressions of sectarian moralism which span the political gamut. Its adherents are equally convinced that they are in the right, equally scornful of the politics of compromise. They see themselves engaged in a Manichean struggle between the "children of light" and the "children of darkness." The latter might be "atheistic Communism" as readily as nuclear power or the teaching of biological evolution. Such a struggle is seen as a game of zero sums in which only total victory by the virtuous, and, therefore, total defeat of the wicked, are possible.

When such people venture into social, political or economic analysis, they are likely to adopt what has been called "the strategy of expecting the worst." As Columbia economist William Vickrey observes:

> To act as though "nature" (or Congress) were an adversary determined to do you in, is, as Samuelson has remarked, as good a definition of paranoia as any, to say nothing of the hubris involved in assuming that your own interests are all that important in the general scheme of things.[8]

Liberation Theology

During the civil rights and anti-war movements of the 1960s the general progression from optimism to pessimism and paranoia was dramatic. Impatience with the tempo of political change led many to adopt a radical stance. And as radicals saw the indefinite postponement of revolution, their radicalism often gave way to embittered defeatism.

To bracket radicalism with other forms of moralism is in no sense to reject a politics of radical social change, or to cast aside the tools of radical social analysis. Certainly the wealth of ideas bequeathed by Marx and some of his interpreters has been of immeasurable help to oppressed peoples in the task of social analysis from *their* perspective or, as theologians of liberation put it, "from below." While that amorphous mass of ideas called Marxist can surely not be defined as God's ultimate truth, it has served as an effective tool of understanding and a sign of worldly hope for many who for reasons of race, class, gender or ethnicity experience oppression and exploitation. The fact that those in power do not like this analysis is in no sense a test of its accuracy. Indeed, it is because oppressed peoples are enabled to see their social position so clearly through the Marxist lens that the privileged find Marxism so threatening.

A critique of radicalism, therefore, is decidedly not a rejection of important criticism by the adherents of theological radicalism: namely, that historically the church, both overtly and covertly, has tended to legitimize the social *status quo*. It is in this connection that the "pedagogy of the oppressed" is a necessary corrective. Nanking theologian K.H. Ting has delivered from inside revolutionary China a trenchant critique of the role played by Christianity within Western capitalist society. In a recent sermon he presents eloquently the position of the world's oppressed:

> [Man] is not only the sinner but also the sinned against, not only the violator of God's laws, but also the violated against, and . . . the task of evangelism is not just to convict man of sin, but to stand alongside man, the sinned against of our society, to feel with him, to be for him.[9]

He continues:

> The beggars need to know that their hunger, their diseases, their sleeping on sidewalks, their infant mortality, their unemployment, their begging, are all of them not the will of God but the result of the greed for power and money on the part of a few and the result of their own passivity. We must help the beggar to see it is not the will of God for him to be so degraded and for his lot to be begging while a few at the top of society are running everything, enjoying all the good things of life and out of their wealth giving alms to beggars. It is only when men and women the sinned against become our concern that God can put in our mouths his word of witness to Christ the saver of sinners. Only then we can speak with authority and the common people will hear us gladly.[10]

The problem arises when radicalism *as ultimate faith* is allowed to replace radicalism *as penultimate politics*. It is the equating of salvation with political liberation, of conscientization* with evangelism, of righteousness with justice, that is fraught with danger. In such an equation both sides lose. Politics becomes a holy struggle ultimately requiring an uncompromising total commitment. The political ethic of liberation is replaced with an all-or-nothing stance in which the human household could be destroyed in the name of saving it. In the laying of so crucially important a corrective on the conscience of Western Christianity, liberation theology may at the same time have substituted another distortion of the Christian witness.

The program of liberation theology consists of three elements: (a) identification of the oppressed; (b) ascribing to the oppressed a special clarity of vision regarding the action of God in history; and (c) founding of a theological/political ethic on vindication and guilt. These elements will be explored in greater detail:

Seeking out the oppressed. This process has an abstract quality that bears little relation to a biblical view of the world in which good and evil are seen as inextricably mixed and intertwined. It may even divert attention from the task of combating genuine oppression where and when it occurs. Furthermore, it divides people against one another as they seek to determine who are the truly oppressed. There is the very real danger that identifying the

---

*A term of liberation theology, and of Paulo Freire in particular, describing the process by which oppressed people come to see their situation, its causes, and the possibility of radical political action to change it.

oppressed can become an elitist pastime, and that privileged persons—guilty in their privilege—may then try to assuage their guilt by facilitating class conscientization on the part of the less privileged. It is perhaps significant that many of the leaders in liberation movements are clergy—members of a privileged group, and beneficiaries of a tradition of aristocratic learning. The pedagogy of the oppressed often involves the prompting of privileged pedagogues.[11]

There is a parallel here with the rhetoric of Islamic militancy in Iran: "There can only be one party in Iran, the Party of the Disinherited, the Party of God."[12] It is thus that liberation rhetoric, fixing on "those of low degree" of whose exaltation Mary sang (Luke 1:52), either ignores the fact that these lowly ones are to be understood as Israel, or else equates all the oppressed with the Israel of God, making oppression a chief mark of the church.[13]

The message of the oppressed. To maintain that oppressed people are unique bearers of the divine Word is to ignore the historical evidence that when the oppressed have gained power, they themselves have often become oppressors. Oppression is rarely ennobling and, except in the case of extraordinarily gifted persons, does not bring one closer to God. The redneck Klansman, for example, reacts against oppression by seeking to oppress others. Afrikaners remember the brutality of their British masters as they, in turn, oppress black people. Lamentably, oppression teaches oppression more often than it does compassion.

Reinhold Niebuhr's analysis of the ethical attitudes of the proletarian classes is at once more realistic and more helpful than that of the liberationists. That analysis suggests that the poor and underprivileged are likely to embody both a moral cynicism that suspects the rhetoric of the self-appointed moral teacher as a mask for self-serving power, and a moral idealism capable of galvanizing political movements for social change.[14] Niebuhr had no illusions about the self-serving tendency of people in *any* social position to justify themselves in moral terms. And he appreciated the irony of history in which the struggle for good (in this case, liberation) so often yields to its opposite (oppression).

To cast oppressed persons in the role of Christ figures, as was done with Caesar Chavez by some of his middle-class sympathizers, is to render a real disservice. Such idealization limits the range of available political choices. It is significant though hardly surprising that when he began to consolidate his position as a union leader, Chavez came under heavy criticism from his middle-class "radical" support.

The politics of guilt. The inducement of guilt, the identification of the guilty, and the rhetoric of vindictiveness, while they are a real part of the continuing struggle within the world, provide a false foundation for a Christian political ethic. It is not because they are *guilty* sinners that Christians participate in the struggle for justice, but because they are *forgiven* sinners. They are not motivated by a desire to serve "Christ the patient"; rather, it is the empowerment of "Christ the agent" that impels them into the arena of political action.

The endless analysis, the identification of "devils," and the politicizing of the eschatological make for a lack of realism that, though it may win battles and even revolutions, is incapable of constructing and governing a society and its economy. The ethos of liberationism, while proclaiming a much needed critical message, promises little in the way of an alternative to the systematic oppression of which it is itself a symptom. As long as "the new man" is understood to be a *political possibility* rather than a *theological reality,* so long the proponents of political salvation will meet with disappointment and deception. Liberation, thus understood, can only be a euphemism for a new kind of oppression.

CHAPTER 4

Another Look at Matthew 25

Evangelical ethics, in its zeal to be true to the witness of Holy Scripture, must be especially attentive to the discipline of hermeneutics: searching out the original meaning of biblical texts and applying that meaning to contemporary life in a way that does not do violence to the text, its original setting or the contemporary scene. Such study presupposes the living, dynamic quality of history; and it resists the temptation of rigid literalism.

The desire for certainty is, of course, an abiding human trait, a manifestation of the basic anxiety that is a part of our finite freedom. We want to be free of our limits; yet we fear both the freedom we do have and its ultimate limit, death. In our uncertainty we desire absolute certainty.

That such desire can become all-consuming and lead to the construction of intricate systems of thought has already been discussed, particularly in connection with moralism. Within the Christian community the need for such escape from freedom manifests itself with particular intensity in the misuse of the Bible.

It is a safe guess that Matthew 25:31-46 is among those New Testament passages most frequently cited in connection with Christian obligation toward the needy, whether in terms of justice or benevolence. The present chapter argues that the traditional interpretation of that passage is not correct: that it violates the basic principles of textual criticism and, in its application, contributes to the perpetuation or even compounding of injustice. The chapter concludes that Matthew 25 should no longer be used to undergird homiletic exhortations on justice or benevolence.

The larger purposes of this chapter are to show, in terms of Matthew 25, the following:

1. The importance of the starting point from which scriptural interpretation is undertaken

2. The way in which a false starting point has led to interpretations which are both untrue to the witness of Scripture itself and supportive of various systems of human behavior which have grown out of that interpretation

3. How pious habit can perpetuate an essentially incorrect biblical interpretation even among persons who otherwise affirm the authentic biblical message

The Starting Point

Evangelical theology understands Scripture to be the written precipitate of the church's living witness to the saving activity of God. The Bible is both the result of that witness and the standard by which the continuing proclamation of the church is to be judged. To be interpreted correctly the Bible must be interpreted from within the historic community of faith under the guidance of the Holy Spirit.

The church cannot, however, claim infallibility for its interpretation of Holy Scripture at a given time and place in history. Within a dynamic pluralism of experience and insight God's Spirit enables the community of faith to correct and refine its understanding of the Scriptures. And the Spirit works throughout the history of God's people, as one generation of Christians studies and clarifies the testimony of another in the light of the divine action to which all bear witness.[1] Every generation of interpreters is obligated to search out and honor the original intent of the biblical writer(s). That original intent is the standard by which all interpretation is to be judged.

The church is free to affirm that the biblical writings are historical in the fullest sense: that they share the ambiguity and "hiddenness" of all historical documents, reflect the influences of the social and cultural settings in which they were written, and are as subject to scientific, literary and contextual analysis as any other such documents. Christians should welcome any analysis which, while itself bound by history, and therefore subject to correction, can be a means of the clarifying work of the Spirit within the community of faith.

Christians are free to adopt such a stance toward scriptural interpretation in the same way that they are free to take non-legalistic and non-moralistic positions concerning such issues as economic justice:

1. They have been liberated from sin, death and the Evil One through God's living, personal encounter in Christ.
2. They have been set free to love their neighbors in the world, using the gifts of reason and common sense.

3. They are therefore free of the need for a sourcebook of moral precepts.

The church perceives the whole biblical message to be a witness to God's loving action in Christ, and the call for response to that action. This response of faith is *participation in the loving action of God for the neighbor's sake*. It is *not* the use of the neighbor as a means of either finding or worshiping God. Christian love participates in the work of "Christ the agent," reaching out to one or many neighbors.[2] It is motivated by the prior liberation of the sinner and thus stands in contrast to an ethic motivated by guilt, in which "Christ the patient," veiled in the needy neighbor, elicits an act of love to God. It is in the light of this total understanding that passages such as Matthew 25 are to be interpreted.

An Inverted Ethic

That Christian preaching and piety should have continued to reinforce the ethic of love to God through Christ the patient even after Luther's recovery of Paul's original message, is due in large part to the persistence of certain pious interpretations which have served as cherished icons up to the present day. Such fundamental errors of biblical interpretation may even have perpetuated the notion that, whatever the relationship between poverty and riches may be empirically, poverty is a necessary part of the divine economy theologically.

Perhaps the most blatant example of this kind of misinterpretation is the frequent reading of Jesus' casual observation at the anointing in Bethany (Mark 14:7; Matt.

26:11; John 12:8) as a decree or mandate. Jesus observes in Mark that "you always have the poor with you, and whenever you will, you can do good to them; but you will not always have me." He thus rebukes the disciples for their hypocritical invocation of the poor in order to criticize the woman's show of devotion. But casual interpreters too frequently quote only the first clause, reading it as though "shall" or "must" were a part of the phrase, as if to say, "You *must* always have the poor with you."

Such a reading misses the meaning of the episode, namely, that the anointing is both a spontaneous expression of devotion and a sign of Jesus' imminent death. Instead, it reinforces a quietism that accepts poverty as a part of the divine order of things.

The Last Judgment

Far more insidious is the popular misreading of Jesus' depiction of the Last Judgment. Matthew places this passage—not a parable in the strict sense—in the context of a private discussion with the disciples on the Mount of Olives following an appearance in the Temple. It is the last in a series of sayings concerning the end of the age and the appearance of the Son of man. These sayings are, in effect, warnings by Jesus to the disciples (and thus, for Matthew, to the church) counseling preparedness and faithful stewardship. Jesus describes the final travail (chap. 24) and admonishes the disciples (and through them the Christian community) to remain watchful and diligent during the time of waiting.

The discourse takes the form of a response by Jesus to questions concerning the signs of the coming of the Son of man. The section contains the parable of the talents, the parable of the ten maidens and the story of the Last Judgment (the latter two of which appear only in Matthew).

In the parable of the ten maidens the faithful are represented as the wise: well-prepared for the bridegroom's coming; neither distracted nor lax because his arrival is delayed. The foolish maidens represent those members of the church whose watchfulness and readiness "ran out" like the oil in their lamps. The parable is clearly addressed to a community which, in addition to being under external stress, is internally beset with questions about the Lord's return. "Watch," Jesus tells them, "for you know neither the day nor the hour" (v. 13).

The parable of the talents is likewise an admonition. It suggests, like the previous parable, that some members of the church, if they are not hopeful and bold in investing of themselves and their substance for the Kingdom's sake, will be found worthless servants (v. 30).

A Concluding Reassurance

With the Last Judgment, however, the message to the church—contrary to popular belief—does not admonish. Rather, it seeks to comfort. The disciples—and therefore the church—are assured that amid all their adversities in an essentially hostile world, it is *through them* that the unbelieving nations will be judged by the Son of man:

> When the Son of man comes in his glory, and all the angels
> with him, then he will sit on his glorious throne. Before him
> will be gathered all the nations, and he will separate them one
> from another as a shepherd separates the sheep from the
> goats, and he will place the sheep at his right hand, but the

goats at the left. Then the King will say to those at his right hand, "Come, O blessed of my Father, inherit the kingdom prepared for you from the foundation of the world; for I was hungry and you gave me food, I was thirsty and you gave me drink, I was a stranger and you welcomed me, I was naked and you clothed me, I was sick and you visited me, I was in prison and you came to me." Then the righteous will answer him, "Lord, when did we see thee hungry and feed thee, or thirsty and give thee drink? And when did we see thee a stranger and welcome thee, or naked and clothe thee? And when did we see thee sick or in prison and visit thee?" And the King will answer them, "Truly, I say to you, as you did it to one of the least of these my brethren, you did it to me." Then he will say to those at his left hand, "Depart from me, you cursed; into the eternal fire prepared for the devil and his angels; for I was hungry and you gave me no food, I was thirsty and you gave me no drink, I was a stranger and you did not welcome me, naked and you did not clothe me, sick and in prison and you did not visit me." Then they also will answer, "Lord, when did we see thee hungry or thirsty or a stranger or naked or sick or in prison, and did not minister to thee?" Then he will answer them, "Truly, I say to you, as you did it not to one of the least of these, you did it not to me." And they will go away into eternal punishment, but the righteous into eternal life. (RSV)

The interpretation of the passage hinges on the meaning of "all the nations" (v. 32) and "these my brethren" (v. 40). That meaning, in turn, requires a grasp of the context which led Matthew to write his Gospel. While such a contextual understanding is essential for the serious interpretation of any passage, it is especially crucial for a proper interpretation of the Last Judgment. Had the passage appeared in one or both of the other synoptic Gospels, perhaps in slightly different settings, a greater breadth of interpretation might be possible. This, however, is not the case. The passage is exclusively Matthew's, and its features are continuous with those which make that Gospel unique.

Matthew's Purpose

Matthew's basic purpose, like that of the other evangelists, was both kerygmatic and churchly. The writers of the Gospels were intent on preserving the Good News of the Risen Lord in a way that would provide a standard against which the church could test its ongoing proclamation. And each wrote in ways that answered the specific needs of the community of Christians that was his particular audience. This approach made each Gospel unique.

The historical setting against which Matthew wrote was particularly grim. The Jewish rebellion of A.D. 66-70 had ended with the destruction of the Temple. In A.D. 73 a few remaining Jewish zealots took their lives at Massada rather than surrender to the conquering imperial forces. After a period of civil turbulence in the empire, a time of persecution of the Christians began under the reign of Domitian. Internally the Christian community was beset with doubts about the Lord's return, problems of discipline, and class divisions. These difficulties are reflected in writings other than Matthew, notably James and Hebrews.

Matthew's distinctive concerns were: (a) to confirm a community of the faithful in their belief that they were, indeed, God's new covenant people; (b) to establish that the church now held the authority first conferred by the Lord on the disciples to interpret, teach and discipline; and (c) to set guidelines for organization and structure within the church, and for the disciplining of its members.

There is considerable evidence of these purposes in Matthew's Gospel. It is the only one in which the term "church" appears: once in the commissioning of Peter (16:18) and once in connection with the disciplining of offenders (18:17). In this Gospel the disciples are portrayed less ambiguously than in the others, with a downplaying of their weaknesses. And the sayings of Jesus are arranged as a "little Pentateuch."

Matthew seems eager to undergird the confidence of the infant congregation for which he writes. It is the members of the Christian fellowship who are the "peacemakers" to be called "children of God" (5:9). They are the "meek" who will "inherit the earth," the despised and persecuted whom their Lord calls "blessed" (5:5, 10ff.).

The members of the Christian community are for Matthew "these little ones" who are not to be despised or made to stumble. A "cup of cold water" given to them will, in fact, be a service rendered to their Lord (18:5,10,14; 10:40-2).

Finally, it is the community of the faithful (those who faithfully keep the Lord's commandments) whom Jesus calls "my brethren" (12:48ff.; 19:29).

As to "all the nations" (25:32), it is they who in Jewish apocalyptic will be judged by the Son of man and the Elect of God whom he represents (Daniel 7:13-15). So now it is Jesus' disciples (and thus, for Matthew, the church) who are to participate in judging "all the nations" who had hated the church (24:9) and its proclamation to them (24:14). Again, let it be emphasized that it is the non-believing *nations,* not all persons generally who are being judged.

So when "the righteous" ask "Where were you . . . and we . . . ?" it is not the pious self-effacement of Christians, but rather the surprised disbelief of tolerant and comparatively humane pagans benignly oblivious of the Christians living in their midst. It is they who have kept Torah, albeit unwittingly. It is for them that the Kingdom has been prepared because of the kindness they extended to "these my brethren."[3]

Many of the standard expositors take offense at this interpretation. It is sufficiently disturbing that Jesus is depicted as a stern judge; but that the church, composed of sinners, should be the means of judging is to them quite unthinkable. It seems to knock away the key support for benevolence to the poor, the stranger and the imprisoned.

Matthew, however, is writing for a church under severe stress. His portrayal of the church is consistent with the rest of his Gospel and altogether appropriate for the occasion. That the early propaganda literature of the Christian movement should contain a strain such as this is hardly surprising. To try to bury it would be more than merely sentimental; it would be dishonest. As for the exercise of hospitality, benevolence and justice by Christians, there are many instances in the New Testament calling for such deeds as expressions of the new life in Christ.[4]

A Shift in Interpretation

The interpretation of "these my brethren" and "all the nations" was shifting as early as the second century toward an understanding of Matthew 25 as an admonition to Christians. By the time of Augustine the conventional interpretation was firmly established: Christians were now being exhorted to act as the "sheep" lest the Kingdom be taken from them.

This shift doubtless resulted from the changed position of the Christian community in the general society, as well as a gradual forgetfulness of the living context to which the passage was originally addressed. The Gospels acquired a literalistic authority for the life of Christians and the church that often bore little relationship to their historic origins. Biblical interpretation was not rooted in primitive Christian struggles, but rather in the condition of the contemporary church. This was especially true of the highly dramatic stories which, like the Last Judgment, became etched in the popular consciousness.

According to conventional interpretations, "these my brethren" is understood to be *anyone in need* rather than the church; and "all the nations" is seen in universal terms, that is, *all of humankind*. It then follows that everyone is or will be judged by his or her deeds of mercy (or the lack of them) toward those in need.[5] Hence the countless pre-Advent sermons warning Christians that they, like everyone else, will be judged by their works. Somehow—to the confusion of the few parishioners who manage to heed the apostolic admonition to stay awake—justification by grace takes a holiday when the Gospel for the Day depicts the Last Judgment.

Who are these brethren in even the least of whom the Son of man is present to receive services of kindness? The standard answer, "anyone in need," has led to innumerable sermons about receiving Christ unawares, the incognito Jesus, and Christ in the faces of the poor. A typical example is Eliza S. Alderson's hymn, "Lord of Glory":

> Wondrous honor you have given
> To our humblest charity
> In your own mysterious sentence,
> "You have done it all to me."
> Can it be, O gracious Master,
> That you deign for alms for sue,
> Saying by your poor and needy,
> "Give as I have giv'n to you."[6]

Thus the poor are channels for "gifts and off'rings due by solemn right" to Christ. And Paul's doctrine of "faith active in love" is replaced by the concept of a Christ who receives the good works of persons through the mediation of the poor and needy. *Christ the agent* of divine love through the believer is replaced by *Christ the patient*. Moreover, Christ's judgment on the negligent is mediated through the same poor and needy. These unserved ones are thus vindicated at the triumphal appearing of the Son of man.

This interpretation had become so imbedded in Christian thinking that not even the Reformers called it into question. Though they sought to read the passage in the light of salvation by grace alone *(sola gratia),* thereby departing from the meritorious works interpretation of medieval theology, the Reformers nonetheless perpetuated the theme of Christ the patient.

Luther in his Large Catechism cites Matthew 25:46,47 to undergird his assertion that the failure to do acts of kindness is equal to murder.[7] In the Apology to the Augsburg Confession, the good deeds of "the sheep" are interpreted to mean the fruits of faith in Christ.[8] That interpretation is also set forth in Luther's commentary on the Sermon on the Mount in which "works of mercy" are seen as evidence of a pure heart, that is, a heart filled with faith in Christ.[9] And in a Christmas sermon Luther declares such deeds as appropriate gifts for the infant Jesus:

> We can offer our gifts just as the Lord says: "Inasmuch as ye have done it unto one of the least of these my brethren, ye have done it unto me." Anybody who gives his goods to the poor, to send children to school, to educate them in God's Word and the other arts that we may have good pastors—he is giving to the Baby Jesus. Jesus was not only born poor and humble but, on account of Herod, had to flee the country. On the journey into Egypt, the presents of the wise men must have come in very handy. In our day too we should not forget those who are suffering.[10]

Among contemporary Lutheran interpretations, Helmut Thielicke's is especially interesting. Thielicke declares the passage to be, in effect, an exhortation to the Christian "to see in his neighbor the veiled Lord."[11] The believer is "obliged to recognize Christ in his neighbor,"[12] to see the person in need as possessing an "alien dignity"[13] by virtue of the Lord's presence in him. Not only does Thielicke perpetuate the motif of "Christ the patient," he contends that the passage calls for a recognition, a "seeing" of Christ who, to the eyes of faith, is no longer incognito. The theme of *finding Christ* overshadows that of *being* or *mediating* Christ.

A Succession of Misreadings

Although this interpretation has persisted for centuries with little variation, it has nevertheless been used to bolster a number of quite different approaches to Christian ethics: (a) the meritorious works ethic of the late medieval church; (b) the marks of election ethic of Westminster Puritanism; (c) the duty ethic of the nineteenth century; and (d) the vindication of the oppressed motif of present-day liberation theology. The interpretation has thus moved from saving works of love done to Christ, to righteous acts performed by God's elect, to the proper benevolence of the good bourgeois, to the judgment of the poor directed at the unjust oppressor. In all these, however, one element has been constant: a love-to-God-through-neighbor ethic which exalts personal benevolence over justice.

1. *The political economy of feudalism*. The conventional interpretation of the Last Judgment was one of the major hermeneutical props for a stable view of a society in which every class, including the poorest, had its proper place ordained by God. In the spiritual economy of the Middle Ages the poor were considered God's gift to the pious, affording the opportunity of earning merits through kind deeds.

The iconography of the time, depicting Christ as the stern judge of all humanity, gave visible reinforcement to this view. It was fear of condemnation as much as love of the Lord that moved people to give alms to beggars. And the monastic movement through which people were enabled—in isolation from the world—to practice faith, hope and love, devoted much of its attention to providing hospitality and care for strangers and the sick. Meanwhile, begging friars institutionalized the opportunity for benevolence on the part of lay persons. All of this transpired under the piercing eye of Christ, seated upon the rainbow, judging humankind by its works or the lack of them.

2. *The marks of the righteous.* In a later time the bourgeois Protestant could take comfort in the knowledge that his or her benevolent deeds were a sure sign of election; and that God in his infinite wisdom had arranged for the presence of the poor on whom the wealthy could bestow some of their surplus. Little heed was paid at first—though later much resistance was given—to the suggestion that the poor might be more justly served by certain basic changes in the structure of the society.

3. *The individualist error.* The idea that human need ought chiefly to be served through individual benevolence runs as a continuous thread through medieval and Protestant thought. The needy were to be served by charity, which was the expression of an impulse of the heart. A rational concept of distributive justice, implemented by the power of the state, is even now resisted by some Christians. The idea of needy people appropriating through revolution the necessities of a dignified life is generally rejected by the affluent.

4. *The piety of the guilt trip.* While the fear-inducing woodcuts of the Last Judgment no longer haunt people's consciousness, the soulful gaze of underfed waifs from the Third World has that power today. Contributors to children's funds and adoption schemes buy satisfaction through their giving. Having relieved their guilt they go their way, giving scant thought to the political and economic structures that permit—perhaps even cause—the miserable conditions under which such children exist.

Such spurious charity drains human energy away from the political task of social and economic change, and helps perpetuate a political economy of which poverty is a necessary component. The meritorious charity of medieval feudalism is replaced by "analgesic" charity. In both cases the poor serve the needs of the rich.

Matthew 25 and Liberation Theology

The theology of liberation is curiously ambivalent in its reading of the Last Judgment. On the one hand there is Gutierrez who categorically rejects the interpretation of "these my brethren" as Christians.[14] Instead, he embraces the Augustinian love-to-God-through-neighbor interpretation.[15] Christ is "Christ the patient." The neighbor is the means through whom the Christian finds, knows and serves Christ.[16] Service to Christ in the neighbor is the evidence of faith, not the unwitting service of the non-believing nations. Indeed, such service when rendered with abandon is a kind of lottery in which the Christian "goes for the big one": fellowship with Christ.[17]

On the other hand, liberationist thought at times seems to identify "these my brethren" with the church, albeit a church with marks that are quite different from the classic ones. Liberationists seem to equate the oppressed class with God's people in our day.[18] A state of oppression, not baptism, is evidence of divine election and a necessary qualification for doing theology. The status of being oppressed is thus made a mark of the true church. The oppressors are consigned to perpetual guilt before the Lord's righteous judgment executed by the oppressed through political revolution. Such revolution is the proleptic foretaste of the final vindication of all oppressed peoples in the appearing of the Son of man.

According to liberation theology the oppressed have the clearest understanding of the Lord's will, for Christ is always on their side. So, as they do theology by action/reflection "from below" the oppressed are, in effect, exercising the office that is given them in Matthew 25: to be the means through which Christ executes his righteous judgment on their oppressors. This orientation also informs the liberationist reading of the Magnificat (Luke 1:46-55) in which "those of low degree" (v. 52) are simultaneously Israel, the church and the oppressed class.

In North America the contemporary heirs of the nineteenth century duty ethic find in Matthew 25 a source of their guilt as oppressors while cheering on the revolution that will sooner or later displace them. Meanwhile they declare their unequivocal solidarity with the oppressed. Thus many "radical" Christians build a sentimental politics of liberation upon a foundation of guilt, unwittingly sharing common ground with the appeal for charity through the eyes of the starving waif.

The liberationist interpretation of Matthew 25 is but the latest version of a persistent misreading of both that passage and the Christian message itself. It reinforces a Christian-neighbor-God orientation, presents a sectarian vision of the church and falsely links earthly liberation with eternal salvation. The true church is seen as a political movement, and Christ's redeeming work as a political program.

Conclusion

The misinterpretation of Jesus' portrayal of the Last Judgment is only one example of the way in which moralistic theology and biblicist piety can distort the church's witness in matters of social justice, directing attention to the alleviation of the symptom rather than concentrating on systematic efforts to correct the cause. The biblical themes of active neighbor-love (Luke 10:25-37) and the doing of justice in response to God's deliverance should provide the Christian with more than sufficient grounding for a committed involvement in the human struggle against poverty and oppression. They express the divine power which liberates Christians and the church to do what is required of good stewards, without the fetters of ideological rigidity or enervating guilt, for the well-being of all the bearers of God's holy image.

CHAPTER 5

An Evangelical Approach

As the foregoing discussion suggests, evangelical ethics prohibits any escape—whether in the form of biblical literalism, moral legalism or ideological absolution—from the responsibility for doing justice in a world of ambiguity and change. Let us turn now to an examination of the arena within which responsible action can take place.

The Context

In the following discussion two points will be argued: (1) that evangelical ethics vigorously affirms the essential unity of economics, politics and ethics; and (2) that it denies with equal vigor the existence of fixed biblical norms which can be applied to specific economic situations at given historical moments. From this it follows that, while on the one hand the clergy cannot make prescriptive statements about economic justice based on direct revelation, yet on the other hand economics is too important to be left solely to the economists. Evangelical ethics thus rejects both clericalism and professional elitism, both theocracy and technocracy, affirming instead that all God's people are equipped and commanded to seek justice together. The church is commanded to be "salt," "leaven" and "light" in the world, activating and encouraging the human family in its quest for justice; and ministers of the Word are called to equip the entire people of God for this servant role.

Biblical faith provides a theological context for ethical judgments in the economic as in other human spheres. However, the literal words of Scripture cannot be used to legitimize any particular economic arrangements. The Bible is to be understood as an organic whole: the witness to God's saving activity. Ethics is done in the context of that understanding. Using the Bible as a sourcebook of truths taken out of the context of the whole is not valid.

The biblical witness does indeed set forth the divine mandate for justice; but it sets forth no blueprint for a just society. It tells us that God cares about the well-being of all the human community (Deut. 10:18,19). It does not tell us how or through what mechanisms or institutions limited resources are to be allocated among those in need of them. It commands us to use our property for the benefit of all, particularly the weakest and poorest (Deut. 24:19-22); but it does not prescribe how this command is to be carried out in a complex industrial society. It demands fairness and honesty in economic relations (Amos 8:4-6); but it does not tell us how to organize the banking system. The widow and orphan are to be cared for (Deut. 24:19-21; Isa. 1:17; Jer. 7:6); but the means for doing so are not fixed. In short, the Bible declares God's will for an open inclusive human family, and the divine command to be fair stewards of the gifts of creation for the benefit of all. But it does not dictate the means: "Who appointed me to be divider between you?'' Jesus asked the quarreling heirs (Luke 12:14). Jesus' calling was to proclaim the reign of God under which all else is judged. Christ's office is to liberate people for faithful living in anticipation of the Kingdom's fruition.

Ethics must recognize the intellectual validity of economics just as it must pay heed to the realities of political power. It must resist the temptation to seek simplistic moralistic solutions to complex problems. At the same time it is obligated to seek out hidden assumptions in technical discourse, and to cut through obscure technical language that may legitimize unjust economic arrangements.

In short, the Lord's command to *do* justice is clear and inescapable. It is the *implementation* of justice that is left to us, God's human family: a family which, though sinful, continues to reflect, however dimly, the image of the Creator. God's concern for his creation is evident in his passion for justice. His love for humankind is seen in his respect for human freedom. It is the human family which must decide how justice can best be done. There is no Christian economics, but Christians must be involved in economic affairs for the sake of that justice which God commands.

Basic Orientation

In approaching any dimension of human life, evangelical ethics begins by affirming the Lordship of the triune God. It presupposes the action of God which both enables and corrects or refines all human efforts to diagnose or prescribe. The work of the Christian is not a matter of seeking God, or discerning God in the face of the neighbor in a believer-neighbor-God sequence. Rather, it is participating in the flow of God's love through persons and human institutions to the neighbor, both in an individual and a collective sense. Evangelical ethics asks, "What best serves my neighbor's need?"

The evangelical ethic is not based on guilt. It is the free action of the new person in Christ who has been liberated from sin, death and the power of the Evil One. Nor is it sectarian. It requires neither a morally perfect people set apart from the world, nor the imposition of specially revealed norms on the world. The neighbor is not provided by God so that we may assuage our guilt and achieve righteousness; rather, the neighbor is the end and object of God's love. And it is that love—expressed socially as justice—that we as believers are set free to express.

But the love of God is not exclusively meted out by the church. It is also mediated through persons and human agencies quite apart from faith. There is no Christian justice or Christian economics any more than there is a Christian mathematics or geography. The Christian person affirms and gives thanks for the Creator's care of the world. The person of faith participates, together with all others of good will, in responding to human need.

Dependence and Interdependence

All human striving and all human claims are made relative by the assertion of faith, that before God persons are due nothing and can make no legitimate demands. We are utterly dependent upon the loving Creator for our being and sustenance. In Luther's familiar words:

> I believe that God has created me and all that exists; that he
> has given and still sustains my body and soul . . . the facul-
> ties of my mind . . . that he provides . . . protects . . . and
> preserves me . . . All this he does out of his pure, fatherly
> and divine goodness and mercy, without any merit or worthi-
> ness on my part. For all this I am bound to thank, praise,
> serve and obey him.[1]

Thus created in dependence on God, we are intended to respond in faith toward God and in love toward one another. It is this capacity for response/responsibility that is the crux of our humanity. Before we are rational or toolmaking or verbal, we are theological beings, created together in the divine image for divine fellowship. Everything that makes us unique as human creatures is intended as a means of responding to God's initiative, or of reflecting the divine image. We are commanded, in Luther's terms, to "fear and love God" by using our human gifts in the service of one another. The refusal so to use these gifts is a manifestation of our lack of faith and trust in God.

Theologically God's questions to Adam and to Cain must be heard together: "Where are you? . . . Where is your brother?" It is in the wilful severing of the relationship of trust and obedience to God that the relationship between brothers and sisters is also destroyed. Standing in a wrong relationship to God, Cain was driven by envy to murder Abel.

Human beings are thus understood by evangelical theology to be created together in the image of God (Gen. 1:27). Mirroring God's image is not the solitary act of each individual. It is the realization of *co*-humanity, and is exemplified by the full "knowledge" of sexual *com*munion. It is in this situation of mutual caring, of accountability to each other and to future generations, that the authentic and living "imaging of God" is done. Conversely, when God's good gifts are used selfishly and worshiped ("graven images," idols), dividing persons against God and each other, the true "imaging of God" is perverted, and co-humanity is destroyed.

Material Interrelatedness

The sexual model of co-humanity is the basis for theological/ethical considerations of economic life. It is here that people make use of things cooperatively to produce the conditions not merely of subsistence, but of meaningful life together. It is here that new generations are born and provided with the material, cultural and spiritual means of carrying on the work of "imaging God." This is the basic meaning of economy *(oikonomia):* ordering the (human) household.

The affirmation of sexuality, productive work and material resources stands in sharp contrast with those philosophies that denigrate the material/temporal character of human life.[2] Thus, the Hellenistic exaltation of contemplation, rest and lack of feeling, coupled with a disdain for physical work, and a denigration of human reproduction, heterosexual love and, therefore, of women, was vigorously opposed by the church.[3] The Apostle Paul, wrongfully branded by many in our day as the original male chauvinist, affirmed material co-humanity (1 Cor. 6:16; 7:2-5); condemned the exaltation of idleness (2 Thess. 3:10); rejected the debasement and perversion of sexuality (Rom. 1: 26; 1 Cor 5:1); and preached the sharing of material resources with those in want (2 Cor. 9). While Christian identity does indeed transcend sexual identification (Gal. 3:28), sexuality is for Paul by no means obliterated by redemption in Christ. Rather, it is a God-given means by which Christians can exercise their calling to servanthood in the world (1 Cor. 7:2-5).

The bias of the technology-based consumer culture against this perception of what it means to be human is a growing challenge to the Christian community. The cult of individual fulfillment is manifested in (1) the separation of biological sex from the context of marriage, and the use of it as a means of pleasure, domination of others, and a symbol of success; (2) the tendency toward a technological sundering of human reproduction and nurturing from sexual co-humanity in the context of the family; and (3) the view of child-bearing primarily as a means to individual self-fulfillment rather than as a contribution to the human family.

The culture of modernity may not share the Hellenistic valuation of contemplation and rest, but it surely promotes an escape from the world, albeit through less sublime means. The sex-oriented advertising, both subliminal and blatant, that helps to power the consumer economy is nothing less than an anti-Gospel of selfish non-responsibility. The use of women as sex objects is the latter-day version of the misogenist bias of Greek culture. The use of marginal persons to do work not yet mechanized corresponds to the Greeks' allocating physical work to women and outcaste Helots or slaves. The pathos of this "economic apartheid" was unforgettably dramatized in the recent film "Bread and Chocolate."

The Community of Work

Work is understood theologically not as individual production and accumulation, but as a social activity which serves to realize and enrich our co-humanity. The division of labor according to efficiency and the diversity of gifts is the means by which "Adam" both cares for and uses the resources of creation (Gen. 2:15). And while human rebellion has brought a curse upon work by making it toilsome (Gen. 3:19, 20), yet the Psalmist celebrates the vestigial goodness of "the work of our hands" (Ps. 90:17).

In the charming film "Lilies of the Field," Sidney Poitier portrays a wandering jack-of-all-trades who, having enjoyed the hospitality of a small community of German nuns in the desert of the American Southwest, decides to express his thanks by building the sisters a chapel. Exuding pride and self-importance, he sets about the project—all by himself. At first a handful and gradually a crowd of Chicanos begins to "hang around" filled with curiosity and not a little envy of the busy Poitier who studiously ignores the spectators. When at length one of them ventures to hand him a brick or tool, he haughtily waves the intruder away. But by then, alone or in twos and threes, the other observers are doing small jobs when he isn't looking, and before he can reverse the tide everyone is at work under his direction! The chapel is completed in a day, and that evening the black foreman, his Chicano crew and the German nuns join in a mass of dedication followed by a fiesta. *Not only has a material project (the chapel) been completed, but co-humanity has been realized in the community of work.*

Sin, Toil and Alienation

Physically demanding or "hard" work should not be viewed as evidence of the curse upon work as a consequence of sin. Indeed, such work can be greatly satisfying, exhilarating and creative of community among those who perform it. The curse on work is seen, rather, in the anxiety attendant upon the struggle for survival, whether "survival" be in terms of the basic necessities of life or the grim competition for status and wealth in the industrialized societies.

Sin is manifested in the compulsion of the "workaholic." It is equally manifested in alienation—the separation of the worker from the control and the rewards of labor, both material and psychic.

Sin is evident in the exploitation of workers by those who own the means of production. Marx's description in *Capital* of the textile mills in nineteenth century Manchester could readily be applied to the illegal sweatshops that exist in America to this day, as well as to their counterparts in such places as the Philippines, Hong Kong and Indonesia. And many American agricultural workers no sooner achieve the fruits of unionization than they find themselves rendered obsolete by labor-saving machines, or crowded out by undocumented alien persons who, having fled poverty in their own countries, become prime targets for exploitation.

Sin is likewise evident in the exclusion of entire groups of persons from employment, or else in their restriction to unrewarding or dead-end jobs. George Bernard Shaw observed that the "haughty American makes the Negro clean his boots, and then proves the inferiority of the Negro by the fact that he is a bootblack."[4] Such attitudes have been eloquently analyzed by Reinhold Niebuhr in his essay "The Ethical Attitudes of the Privileged Classes."[5]

Finally, sin manifests itself in the tendency of some societies to define people in terms of the work they do, their success (as measured by monetary reward) or both. Not only are persons depreciated when forced into idleness, but even voluntary service, because unpaid, is accorded less value. This issue is addressed in the recent statement of the Lutheran Church in America "Aging and the Older Adult":

> People in our work-oriented society tend to view personal dignity largely in terms of occupational performance. As a consequence, loss of occupation or retirement frequently results in the loss of one's sense of dignity. While acknowledging the many problems that arise from unemployment or retirement, this church nevertheless affirms that human dignity has a far deeper foundation than work or status.
>
> God's love for all persons is creative and unconditional. Human beings have dignity not because they have achieved success or the esteem of the world, but because they are made in the image of God.[6]

Christian ethics considers it morally incumbent upon society and the holders of power within it, to strive for a fair structuring of the community of work. Responsible social and corporate policy should aim at distributing opportunities for employment in an equitable fashion that will enhance the dignity of both the worker and the work. All useful and necessary work should be accorded esteem quite apart from financial remuneration, the rung of the job on the career ladder or the degree of physical toil. And the job should be seen as a means by which the worker may enhance the quality of personal, familial and community life.

Technology: A Mixed Blessing

In light of the biblical affirmation of work as an essential mark of humanity, one wonders whether the technological revolution may be speeding us toward a time when productive work by persons will be superfluous. Is the dream of a life without toil propelling humanity toward a point at which consumption will be the sole human activity? In Hannah Arendt's words, will "the age-old dream of the poor and the destitute, which can have a charm of its own as long as it is a dream . . . turn into a fool's paradise as soon as it is realized?"[7] Arendt concludes that a world without work, supported by a technology dedicated to a spurious happiness realized through the satisfaction of artificially contrived needs, will lead to a state of "universal unhappiness."[8]

This sort of technological unemployment would, according to Arendt, lead to a general state of enforced leisure. But since the technologically unemployed already constitute a problem for economists and ethicists it is difficult to see how a non-working society could be a solution—especially if one believes in the positive value of work.

The dream of such a leisure society is highly suspect from a biblical view, for two chief reasons: (1) it denies the creative (and procreative) nature of the body, making it into an organ of pleasure; and (2) it implies consumption of non-renewable resources at a rate contrary to the divine command of stewardship of the earth. The pleasure-

97

oriented society attends to the appetites of the "now generation," and pays scant heed to the just claims of generations to come.

Evangelical ethics normally views technology as a *means* which can be employed for either good or ill. In the prospect just depicted, however, technology would forsake its instrumental function, becoming instead the definer and determiner of humanity, rather than its servant. It is against such an eventuality that the church must constantly be on guard.

Maldistribution and Non-Community

Whatever the likelihood of Arendt's prediction, a clear ethical issue is posed by the disproportionate consumption of non-renewable wealth by the world's technological societies, while the majority of people subsist on the edge of starvation. If not a simple redistribution of wealth, then certainly a redistribution of opportunity, production and technological skills is called for. How this can be achieved in political terms is the difficulty, since development is so closely related to the prevailing values of industrialized societies—values which many Third World societies seek to emulate.

Distribution of wealth will continue to be a problem and its solution will be practical rather than theological. However, theological ethics can state certain principles as guidelines. Too great a disparity of wealth/income, for example, fragments a community, separating the rich from the poor, effectively shielding the more privileged from the care of their needy neighbors: "Out of sight, out of mind." Furthermore, too much power rests in the hands of too few, excluding the many from any effective control over the quality of their own lives. The dehumanizing effects of such disparities are especially evident in the developing countries. However, the developed world is scarcely immune from similar forms of economic Balkanization and disenfranchisement.

The Stewardship of Wealth

Wealth may be defined simply as that which is valued by a society. The discipline of economics defines wealth as including both natural resources and humanly-produced capital. Indeed, Adam Smith saw wealth primarily as the product of human activity, and the means by which further production is possible. The social determination of what in fact is "valuable," and what kind of activity is to be considered productive, illustrates how the economy is imbedded in the cultural and moral consensus of society.

The biblical witness has consistently declared that wealth, however defined, is ultimately a gift of God. No wealth can be produced without the original God-given means of producing it: the myriad resources of the natural world and the human capacity to use them creatively. It is to the responsible stewardship of both this original wealth and derivative, produced wealth that we are called by God.

Biblical faith has viewed the amassing of wealth as a form of both idolatry and theft. The false security of wealth is seen in the parable of the rich fool (Luke 12:13-21) and the destruction of human community through hoarded wealth in the story of Dives and Lazarus (Luke 16:19-31).

As to how (or whether) wealth is to be held, managed and used, Christian thinking has, at best, been ambivalent. Jesus' sayings about the worship of Mammon and the difficulties of the rich who wish to enter the Kingdom, as well as his challenge to the rich young man, have left the faithful uneasy at best. Christians have dealt with such uneasiness in ways that have often had ironic consequences.

In the late Middle Ages those monastic orders dedicated to such ascetic virtues as poverty found themselves showered with gifts from the guilt-ridden nobility. Later the rising merchant-class sought to gain merits for itself by supporting the monks' good works of self-denial, with the result that the monastic orders became embarrassingly rich. This form of doing well by doing good also became the mark of certain Protestants who led unostentatious lives of self-denial while amassing great wealth through hard work and thrift. While Luther and Calvin in a clear carry-over from the medieval canonists denounced usury,[9] their followers, swept along by the commercial revolution, soon forgot the older prohibition, enthusiastically using money to make money.

The relationship between Protestant teaching and capitalism has been the subject of much exploration and debate.[10] Suffice it to say that with the rise of capitalism, unease about wealth gave place to an ethic of accumulation. John Wesley's endorsement has become a classic statement:

> Gain all you can, by honest industry. Use all possible diligence in your calling. Lose no time. If you understand yourself, and your relation to God and man, you know you have none to spare . . . That wherein you are placed, if you follow it in earnest, will leave you no leisure for silly, unprofitable diversions . . . Gain all you can by common sense, by using in your business all the understanding which God has given you.[11]

The Individualist Error

Wesley promoted the idea of *individual* stewardship.[12] He combined the biblical idea of the steward who cares for what is held in trust for another, with a doctrine of individualism and private property borrowed from the Enlightenment. He believed that a person spiritually restored through Christ was capable of the best possible stewardship of private possessions without the taint of selfishness.[13] Wesley believed that self-interest, enlightened by reason and the Gospel, would work for the common good through what Smith had called "the invisible hand."

Thus for Wesley and his followers the *obligation* of individual stewardship before God became the legal *right* of the individual alone to determine the disposition of his or her goods. For Wesley, as earlier for Locke and Smith, economic activity did not include political power, legislation or collective action. Unlike Smith, however, Wesley affirmed the importance not only of individual enterprise but of benevolence as well.

Critical analysis suggests that such an interpretation of stewardship ignores two themes that are central to evangelical ethics: (1) the concept of co-humanity, and (2) the persistence of sin in the regenerate person. In the first instance such individualism denies the concept of mutual accountability within society for the responsible use of its resources. Nor does it concern itself with communal and institutional ways of achieving the best stewardship of limited resources.[14]

Because Wesley's orientation plays down the continuing reality of sin in the redeemed person, it also tends to ignore the tendency of human beings to rationalize their selfishness and self-aggrandizement in terms of piety and benevolence. This view denies the need for correctives through competing power, civil or communal institutions and legislation. In short, it leaves to the individual the sole determination of what constitutes faithful stewardship.

Stewardship and Politics

Stewardship requires means devised and determined by human reason in response to historic circumstances. One of these means, though limited in scope, is the legal concept of private property. Like any other legal/institutional means of stewardship, private property is politically determined. The pattern by which wealth is distributed, managed and held both reflects and determines the distribution of political power within a society. Any change in this pattern is fundamentally political in character.

It is crucial that political institutions and office holders, as they attend to the public weal, include economic well-being within the scope of their concern. In Luther's discussion of the petition for daily bread in the Lord's Prayer he writes the following: "It would therefore be fitting if the coat-of-arms of every upright prince were emblazoned with a loaf of bread instead of a lion or a wreath of rue, or that the loaf were . . . stamped on coins . . ."[15] While the role of the prince was narrowly understood, and "interventionist policies" were not a part of the simple economy of his day, Luther sensed an inevitable relationship between a society's political stance and its economic welfare. By substituting the loaf for the lion, Luther emphasized the ultimate purpose or end of politics, namely, human welfare, rather than the means to that end, power and might.

Determining the values of a society, devising the institutional means by which they are to be achieved, allocating scarce resources, providing for future generations: all these are political functions with a clear economic dimension. Economic activity or the ordering of the human household on all levels—local, national, worldwide—is essentially political. In such activity theology makes no attempt to prescribe specific ways of ordering social and economic relationships, but does insist that such ordering cannot be left to chance. A crowded, hungry and strife-torn planet dare not depend on an "invisible hand."

The principle and the policies of unrestrained increase are no longer adequate. While feeding the hungry and relieving the poor do indeed require economic production, the economic question is not simply "How much?" but "For whom, by whom and how?" The fair allocation of production, the distribution of the economic product, and the consequences of economic choices for the environment and future generations are inextricably linked issues. It is the *quality* of all human life rather than a perpetually higher standard of living for some which must determine current policy and action. Such reorientation cannot be left to chance.

This does not imply, however, the advocacy of a particular political-economic system. The point is, rather, that the systematic separation of politics and economics is a fundamental distortion of the concept of stewardship. An economic system within a society is the result of specific political choices. This is equally true of public decisions concerning the ownership of land, natural resources and capital. The best way of allocating resources and distributing the economic product is an open question theologically; but the requirement of justice for the whole human family is non-negotiable. Theological ethics does not see any one political system as inherently good or bad. Rather, it judges them on the basis of their performance in terms of the general human welfare.[16]

Justice

The ultimate purpose of politics and economics, in terms of evangelical ethics, is human well-being. It is such well-being which, in theological terms, enables persons to reflect the divine image of co-humanity in which they have been created. The classical definition of justice is consistent with this understanding, that is, to give to each that which is due him or which is her own. Justice, in short, is correlative with human need.

Contemporary Western economists such as Hayek and Friedman, following the thought of Locke and Smith, understand justice primarily in formal or legal terms. It is essentially the legal structure which, through enforcement of contracts, restraint of monopolies and provision of equal access to the market, insures the harmonious operation of private enterprise. This understanding is based on the assumption that all the participants have equal advantages and opportunities. This has already been defined as *commutative* justice.

In a world riddled with vast disparities of advantage, a justice which does no more than enforce the rules of a game in which all are presumed to be equal participants is simply not enough. True justice demands compensatory strategies for those who, for a variety of reasons not of their own making, lack what is required for equal participation. Income maintenance, remedial training, transfers of technology, grants-in-aid, and affirmative action in employment are all examples of compensatory strategies.

The just society is one which strives through appropriate legal and administrative means to guarantee to all its members those minimal necessities—defined in terms of specific circumstances and available resources—which enable participation in the society. The ideological opponents of this notion usually argue in terms of merit rather than right, contending that even the basics of life must be earned. Yet, as Franklin D. Fry points out, they themselves generally do their utmost to secure and bequeath unearned advantages to their children.[17]

In terms of evangelical theology, two historic misinterpretations must be corrected if economic justice is to be understood in any fruitful sense: (1) the idea of justice as *mere* justice, and (2) the idea of justice as divine righteousness.

Mere Justice

In the first example justice is ranked as inferior to charity. This is a remnant of medieval thought, which ranked justice together with prudence, temperance and courage as one of the lesser, or "natural," virtues. Charity, on the other hand, together with faith and hope was regarded as "supernatural," or unattainable without grace. Justice, being that which was demanded or expected, had a status inferior to that of charity, which was regarded as especially meritorious because it was done in addition to what was expected. Charity meant "going the second mile."

In its Protestant version "mere justice" is subordinated to the pious conduct of the private individual. Thus Wesley had confidence in the willingness of the conscientious Christian to give all he or she could, without giving thought to the possibility that the person's largesse might be misdirected or used to enhance one's personal power or standing in the community. Justice, on the other hand, was minimal and formal. For justice to assume any function of private benevolence was regarded as an affront both to the rich and to the God who had rewarded their hard work with the means to be benevolent.

It must also be noted that Adam Smith considered "mere justice" (a term he used in *The Wealth of Nations*) to be simply the body of legal obligations undergirding capitalism;[18] that it facilitated the private pursuit of self-interest which, in turn, helped bring about general well-being. Wesley would have agreed. However, he would have assigned a more positive role to private benevolence.

According to evangelical ethics, justice and benevolence (institutionalized as private philanthropy) are both manifestations of God's love for persons. Benevolence, or charity, is defined as a personal act of kindness or good will. That which is done or given out of charity may, however, be something which in any case is due the recipient as a matter of simple justice.

Justice may be defined as *the form of God's love in a finite and sinful world*. Justice is a tangible expression of love when there are many neighbors and limited resources. It is *distributive love*. It is what love demands and may, in fact, enforce through institutions of government when private individuals or communities are unwilling to serve the common good or their needy neighbors. Justice through coercion may require the coercive power of the state or even political revolution when the established government through incompetence, venality or arbitrary rule has abandoned its proper stewardship under God. Justice—manifested in many ways and at many different points in history—is always an expression of the creative and sustaining love of God. To denigrate justice or the means through which it is achieved, therefore, is to belittle God himself.

Justice and Righteousness

While the concept "mere justice" vitiates the "justice-form" of the powerful love of God, there is another misinterpretation that errs in the opposite direction: the equating of justice and righteousness. Exalting justice beyond all human reach is to rob it of all utility as an effective instrument for divine action in a finite and sinful world.

According to evangelical ethics, righteousness denotes the saving love and power of God. It gives to the penitent sinner a new life that bears the fruits of repentance. Righteousness is God's redemptive work. The end of righteousness is *shalom,* "the peace of God that passes understanding." *Shalom* is not a human achievement, or even the result of human/divine cooperation. It is a peace experienced by the believer as a hint of what may be expected in the consummated Kingdom at the blessed appearing of the risen Christ.

The persistent temptation for Christians is to equate righteousness with justice, and to view its final expression, *shalom,* as an achievable utopia. This tendency, endemic to Christianity from its earliest origins, and condemned by the Reformers as a new monasticism,[19] has appeared and reappeared through Christian history, most recently in the forms of anti-technological communalism and liberation theology. The tyranny and the destructive tendencies of a misconceived *shalom* is dramatically illustrated by the tragedy of Jonestown, Guyana. When people seek to turn a saving gift into law, an eschatological promise into a temporal reality, and the peace of God into submission to theocratic rule, the result—both empirically and theologically—can only be tyranny, disillusionment and, ultimately, death. In unadorned Lutheran terms, this world cannot be ruled by the Gospel. It must be ruled by the political use of God's law through the exercise of human power and reason. And the end of law is not salvation, but justice.[20]

Ecological Justice and Reverence for Life

A current pop ethic seeks to extend the dimension of justice to include the natural environment. Concurrently there is a certain ethical strain in the Christian community that persists in assigning ultimate significance to the abstract category "life." The two phenomena are not unrelated, and since both deal with natural (land) and human (labor, human capital)[21] resources, they need to be analyzed in any ethical treatment of economic justice.

Evangelical ethics categorically rejects the resurgence of a pantheistic view of nature, or the basing of an ecological ethic on a "kinship" of creatures bearing the divine image with the rest of creation. As it has been variously asserted in this discussion that *the earth does not belong to humankind* ("The earth is the Lord's and the fullness thereof" Ps. 24:1), so it must now be stated with equal vigor that *humankind does not belong to the earth.* Though made from its elements, human beings are created both to use and care for the earth as children of God, not as sons and daughters of the Great Earth Mother.

It is, therefore, theologically false to assert that in their abuse and plunder of the natural world, people have sinned against the earth. Rather, *they have sinned against God.* Without regard for their neighbors they have stolen, hoarded and exploited God's creation for their own use, violating the divine image of co-humanity. Their desire for dominance without accountability has denied their neighbors the means of being human—of acting as stewards of God's gift. It is not, therefore, justice to nature that is the issue, but a faithful and prudent use and care of nature for the sake of justice to the neighbor. In order to repair the ravages that have been inflicted upon the earth and to strive for its continued nurture and care, we must encourage stewardship for justice.

Similarly, concerning the second point, Christians are called not to revere life but to be stewards of it. "The sanctity of life" is a misleading phrase, for God alone is holy. It is not the profusion of life, but its quality, that should be the concern of faithful stewardship. That such an orientation involves risk should be faced squarely. "Quality of life" has been used by tyrants to justify genocide; and it can as easily be used by the advocates of triage and totalitarian programs of eugenics. But the risk, once recognized, cannot be allowed to frighten us away from an ethic of stewardship. Recognizing risk and guarding against it are, indeed, part of responsible stewardship.

The temptation to act in self-serving ways under the guise of stewardship is always present. A constant re-evaluation of economic decisions is needed to insure that concern for quality of life does not become, in effect, concern for the quality of some people's lives at the expense of others' very existence. Good stewardship demands mutual accountability among the members of the human family. Securing such accountability is a political task that is never complete.

Conclusion

In conclusion let us briefly contrast the evangelical understanding of economic justice with that of the individualism which first grew out of the Enlightenment and has recently been reborn in the form of privatism and self-actualization. Risking the danger of caricature, we will contrast certain evangelical themes with those of life, liberty, property and the pursuit of happiness as expressed by Locke and Jefferson.

For "life" the Christian substitutes material co-humanity: human relationships with concrete moral obligations in a world that is both material and historic. It is not "life" but my *neighbor,* both individually and collectively, whom God wills to love through me.

For "liberty" the Christian substitutes the "glorious liberty of the children of God": the freedom to serve one's neighbor. In secular society, individual liberty is understood as a civil good protected by law. For Christians it is a means for the stewardship of self and one's resources for the sake of the neighbor.

For "property" the Christian substitutes stewardship. Private property in the legal sense is seen as a means of individual stewardship. Good stewardship may dictate that certain property is best held in common for the common good. Persons, individually and collectively, are accountable both to God and neighbor for what they hold in trust—even their own bodies.

For "the pursuit of happiness" the Christian substitutes mutual service. Personal happiness is not understood to be the ultimate goal of the Christian. It is, rather, the by-product of a quite different pursuit: the good of the neighbor.

CHAPTER 6

The Task of the Church

God has provided us with the gifts of reason and common sense so that we ourselves may discover in what specific ways we can best be faithful stewards of resources and political power. As members of the Body of Christ, we are free to engage in the ministry to which, by baptism, we have been ordained. The church, though neither qualified nor called to pronounce any political or economic program as the unambiguous expression of God's will, nevertheless cannot grant to any area of human activity a false autonomy which denies moral criticism.

There are many practical means through which the church can aid in the advancement of economic justice. Any listing must always be open to modification, elaboration and expansion. After all, in the final analysis it is committed people in specific circumstances with particular resources and opportunities who develop the economic agenda of the church. The following functions may suggest possible expressions of the church's servant role in the realm of economic justice:

1. Critic of social convention
2. Clarifier of relevant issues

3. Enabler of people

4. Participant in policy making

5. Manager of resources

Critic of social convention. Criticism is essential for the ongoing life of any person or community. It keeps the future open and flexible by radically questioning in both moral and practical terms the "rightness" of certain modes of behavior, policies or ways of life. While the church affirms that God's criticism or judgment comes from beyond the world, it apprehends and applies that criticism within the world, in the midst of all its ambiguities, *for the sake* of that world which is the subject of God's love.

The critical function for which the church is uniquely qualified is, of course, theological: to remind society that no set of human arrangements, no state and no ideological system is divinely ordained or beyond criticism. It is precisely through such criticism that the church helps the society to free itself of tyrannical domination; to be flexible and open to new challenges; and to avoid making devils of the opposition.

Because it sees itself as a community of liberated people, the church is free not only to challenge unquestioned assumptions but to help the entire society do so. "Why must it be?" or "Is there not a better way?" are questions posed by free people. While the church is not qualified to give final answers, it must, together with all people of good will, pursue such provisional solutions as seem to advance the well-being of the human family.[1]

Clarifier of relevant issues. This function is closely related to that of critic, and may indeed be an aspect of it.

Clarification is, at least in part, analysis and description. While the church has no unique insight into the specifics of a particular historical situation—indeed, it rejects all claims to infallibility in its efforts at diagnosis and analysis—it *does* possess one invaluable characteristic: its inclusiveness.

The church is not guided and motivated by a narrow perception of the world, but by the forgiving and liberating Word. That Word creates open space in which God's people, embracing the full range of human experience, every race and nation, all economic positions and occupations, may discover the specifics of worldly justice. It is within this capacious "house," established and maintained by God's saving activity, that the Spirit is free to enlighten and empower God's people.

The church must nurture that universality and openness, encouraging the entire people of God to participate in the action and reflection that leads to clarity. Such work is never done. The church can too easily become bound by class, culture, or national interest. Only as it strives to express its essential catholicity through inclusiveness can it perform the ministry of critic and clarifier.

Enabler of people. The responsibility to enable or empower was part of the church's task long before these terms achieved currency. As a community or family— particularly as manifested in the life of the local congregation—the church has traditionally provided a supportive context within which people have learned to care for one another, to be self-governing and to organize for specific tasks, especially those related to human welfare.

The church has helped to nurture a culture of civility; it has served to generate political awareness and skill; and it has helped to develop political institutions. This enabling function, which it has performed throughout its history, the church continues to perform in those nations and communities which are now achieving self-determination.

The church nurtures in its members a sense of self-worth and an obligation to service, and through such self-motivated and cooperative individuals it contributes to the general welfare. The promotion of home and family, as well as the cultivation of a sense of the larger human family, has always been a vital part of the church's role as servant to society. Thus, the church exercises its own corporate stewardship and at the same time prepares persons for individual stewardship in their various secular roles.

As enabler, the church may equip persons to resist, replace or transform unjust social institutions. This is exemplified by the "base communities" in Latin America, as well as the close church ties of many nationalist leaders in Africa. Furthermore, the church functions as the "midwife of social change" in impoverished communities within the industrialized world. The whole church, while mindful of the inherent ambiguities and risks, should affirm this aspect of its servant role, and seek ways of making it more effective.

In the impersonal, highly bureaucratized mass societies of the developed world, the church can play a vital mediating role between personal and institutional expressions of political and economic power.[2] Such mediating communities can serve the following functions:

a. To monitor the behavior of government and corporate power, especially as it affects the quality of community life

b. To see to it that those necessities and benefits to which persons are entitled by law are in fact delivered by the agencies which have been mandated to provide them

c. To hold the structures of government and corporate power accountable when they cause injury or damage to persons and communities

d. To create public awareness of issues related to the quality of life, and to help people and communities develop political competence as they address those issues in the realm of public policy

e. To enable people and communities to discover areas in which they can affect the shape and quality of their lives; be self-determining and not totally dependent upon the impersonal agencies of government and corporate power

To varying degrees within industrialized societies people have become accustomed to a life of increasing dependence. The fast food industry is but one conspicuous example of this phenomenon. In nearly all aspects of life people are becoming increasingly passive consumers of processed or pre-cooked goods, values, certain forms of "religion," and a vast array of government services. The rugged individual producer of an earlier day has given place to the passive individual consumer of the present.[3]

This net of dependency spreads as new regions and population groups give up all vestiges of self-sufficiency to become tied into larger systems. The resulting passivity, particularly in terms of psychic dependence, should be a matter of grave concern. The church must seek to recover its historic *capacity to form persons and communities capable of responsible, self-determining stewardship.* It must act as a corrective to both spurious *in*dependence and debilitating *de*pendence, fostering constructive stewardship within an increasingly *inter*dependent world.

Participant in policy making. As a specific dimension of its role as enabler, the church should assume an increasingly significant role in public policy making, based upon the following assumptions:

a. The basic commitment of the church to human well-being rather than to special interest

b. The willingness of the church to put aside all pretense to special knowledge and technical competence, and to participate on an equal basis with all persons and groups committed to justice

c. The recognition by the church that sound public policy requires diligent work in the clarification of issues and articulation of needs by the people whose lives that policy will materially affect

The last of these assumptions is perhaps the most neglected. Accustomed to the role of passive consumer, people in highly developed and bureaucratized countries have come to expect from their governments instant response to instant demand. They fail to see that legislation comes at the conclusion of a long and complex social transaction: the ringing up on the cash register after a lengthy shopping tour. While the church, together with other socially concerned groups, must be an effective participant in the legislative process, such involvement will have limited significance unless the full constituency of the church has shared in the stating of concerns, clarifying of issues, and proper selection of emphases in the interest of good stewardship. Such involvement, when done with care, is cumulative in effect, and can generate a clearly perceived political will that affirms and supports social justice.

Manager of resources. As employer, fund raiser, investor, purchaser and provider of goods and services, and property owner, the church must practice what it preaches in terms of institutional stewardship. Church managers need to express in very practical and basic ways the concern of the church for social justice:

a. Personnel policy and practice, including equal opportunity employment, fair wage/salary policies, training and advancement, and healthful working conditions

b. Use of resources, with special attention toward minimization of waste and environmentally sound consumption

c. Purchase of goods and services from vendors and contractors who support racial justice, human rights, environmental stewardship and other socially constructive policies

d. Use of property, including the selective voting of securities and selective investment policies that reflect the church's commitment to social justice

The Risk of Stewardship

Participation by Christians in the quest for economic justice may be costly and full of risk. Indeed, there are times when Christian faithfulness requires the treading of a veritable knife edge.

Shortly before his still unsolved abduction on July 18, 1979, Gudina Tumsa, General Secretary of the Ethiopian Evangelical Church Mekane Yesus, called upon his brothers and sisters in Christ to adopt a stance of critical solidarity with the whole Ethiopian people during their time of strife and uncertainty. He urged each Christian to go beyond mere payment of taxes to the active investment of "money, time, knowledge and life, as well as anything else he may treasure" in the service of the entire people. Then, in a discerningly pastoral word, Tumsa described the meaning of critical solidarity in the Ethiopian context:

> In the program of the National Democratic Revolution of Ethiopia three arch enemies are listed, namely imperialism, feudalism and bureaucratic capitalism. These are systems to which the Ethiopian masses are firmly opposed. Today "Down with Feudalism," "Down with Capitalism" and "Down with Imperialism" mean simply that as Ethiopians we no longer want to live under these systems. As a matter of fact, feudalism, capitalism and imperialism are things of the past as far as the Ethiopian masses are concerned. There are other numerous slogans that have cropped up during the various stages of the revolution to inspire people and to urge them to do their part with enthusiasm.
>
> Many things were considered "adiaphora" (non-essential for salvation) by the early church. But when it concerned the denial of the Person of Christ as Lord, the believers preferred physical death to earthly life and went for martyrdom. The term martyrdom is derived from a Greek word which means

witness. Martyrdom means a believer witnesses for Christ by dying.

It should be clearly understood that the good news of Jesus Christ can never be seen as a part of the systems that came about at the various stages in the process of historical development in world history. The Gospel is the power of God working in the human heart with a view to transforming man and thereby putting him in a right relationship with God who is the source and goal of his life, regardless of the stage in the process of historical development at which man finds himself. The Christian Gospel refuses to be identified or to be considered as a part of feudalism or capitalism and as such it cannot fade away with these systems, since by its nature the Gospel of Christ is totally different from them. Christ himself is the Gospel. There is no Gospel apart from His presence with us in our daily labor. Christ is the living Lord who was raised from death by God the Father. A living person cannot be identified with any impersonal system. A person can work in any system and the living Lord Jesus Christ commands us to go out and proclaim his presence, the good news. He forgives our sins and saves us from the bitter experiences of sin. Only a living person can perform such things.[4]

This eloquent statement of faithful stewardship and critical solidarity in a situation of extremity is just as applicable in a more settled political and social context. The church—the new people of God in Christ—expresses itself in and through communities and institutions within the world. It is thus that we, as God's people, are called to exercise our stewardship for the sake of justice. God's liberating Gospel enables us to participate fully in "the art of stewarding fairly," even, and especially, when such fairness may challenge some cherished myths and assumptions and cause us to re-examine some previously unquestioned principles.

The Task Before Us

Delegates to the Fourth Assembly of the Lutheran World Federation were asked to ponder the following words: *a world broken by unshared bread*.

It is no longer possible for people and nations to plead helplessness before the whims of nature in the face of persistent human misery. Natural disasters and the accident of geographical location have taken second place to political and economic decisions as factors determining human suffering. Famine caused by natural events has been replaced by starvation resulting from poor stewardship of power, resources and imagination. Whether through the passive acceptance of existing arrangements or by deliberate political choice, *people* are now largely responsible for human suffering and need. The tragedies of Kampuchea, East Timor and Ethiopia, of Soweto and the South Bronx, were not caused by typhoons or earthquakes.

While dreams of the limitless expansion of technology-based affluence may be at an end, human imagination and skill are nevertheless capable of achieving a stewardship of resources and power which can end starvation and misery caused by human error. Such stewardship includes the prudent and just management of resources, production and distribution, as well as the responsible control of human reproduction itself.

It is neither moral nor wise for the affluent sectors of the world to continue equating "standard of living" with "quality of life," while millions of people must exist without the barest necessities. The brokenness of the world by unshared bread is tangible evidence of that sin which separates people from their Creator and from one another. Christians are reminded of this when, having prayed, "Give us this day our daily bread," they immediately say, *"Forgive us our sins."*

God's assurance of forgiveness sets people free to bear the fruits of repentance: to create and exercise the political will that can begin to reunite the entire human family through the sharing of bread. It is to this task that the liberating power of God impels us.

A Social Statement of the Lutheran Church in America

Economic Justice
Stewardship of Creation in Human Community

Adopted by the Tenth Biennial Convention, Seattle, Washington
June 24-July 2, 1980

Introduction

God wills humanity to exercise justice in its stewardship of creation. Holy Scripture declares that the earth is the Lord's, and that persons created in God's image are divinely authorized to care for this earth and to share in its blessings. Since human community is dependent on responsible stewardship, God commands that persons deal equitably and compassionately in their use of the earth's limited resources in order to sustain and fulfill the lives of others.

It is in obedient gratitude for all the gifts of God that we in the Lutheran Church in America commit ourselves in faithful love to struggle for economic justice as an integral part of the witness and work of God's People in the world.

Economy in Society

The word "economy" is derived from the Greek words which mean the ordering of the household. In this basic sense, economy denotes the activity of persons in the management of all the resources (natural, human, and manufactured) of this world.

An economic system is the pattern of relationships, processes, institutions and regulations, together with the values underlying them, by which the activities of production, distribution, and consumption are carried out in and among societies and cultures.

Economic policies and institutions develop through social custom and political decision. The allocation of the resources, burdens, and benefits of the economy is variously done: by traditional habits, by individual choice in the marketplace, by governmental regulation, by the action of corporations, or by all of these. Likewise the institutional constraints on economic activity are made by these means separately or in combination.

Economic activity is embedded in the total life of a society. Relations of production and distribution reflect the prevailing patterns of power as well as the values by which a society lives. The material allocations within a society are both an effect and a cause of the basic character of that society. The economic choices of the members and institutions of a society reflect what a society is and influence what it is becoming.

The fundamental questions underlying any economic system are therefore political and moral in nature. There are always technical questions that are peculiar to the operation of any given system, but the basic issues are not technical in character. For example, who may work? What should motivate our labors? By whom and how should it be decided what to produce, where to distribute, and how much to consume? Who determines, and how, the "fairness" of prices, profits, wages, benefits and strikes? How do we balance economic production and environmental protection? Do our economic practices reflect or reinforce child exploitation, sexism, ageism, racism, or anti-Semitism? The answers, never final, emerge qualified and compromised from the field of contending interests, powers, and moral claims.

The organization of economic life has undergone vast changes throughout the course of history, and no economic "system" has ever shown itself to be permanent. The appearance of new conditions, the development of new technologies, and the evolution of social values and political structures have all occasioned the alteration or replacement of economic institutions and relationships.

126

It is in such a world of continual change, amid graphic evidence of both progress and exploitation, that the Holy Spirit calls the church to bear witness to God's sovereign reign in our midst. As the Lord of history God acts in society to judge and fulfill the daily efforts of all people in their economic theory and practice.

Theological Foundations

All persons are intended to respond in worship and work as one human family to the Creator's love: to propagate, nurture and extend human life and enhance its quality; to protect and use wisely the world's resources; to participate with God in the continuing work of creation; and to share equitably the product of that work to the benefit of all people.

In a world broken by sin the Creator lovingly enables the doing of justice. Into such a world God calls the redeemed in Christ to be advocates and agents of justice for all.

The Image of God

Human life depends totally on a loving Creator. All persons are made in God's image for a life of trust, obedience, and gratitude.

Life under God is also meant to be life in community. There is no humanity but co-humanity, for one cannot be human alone. It is only together that persons can realize their creation in God's image. This image is reflected as persons respond in love and justice to one another's needs. Male and female persons are created equally in the image of God (Gen. 1:27). It is in the basic human relationships of domestic, political, and economic life that persons share in their common humanity. God's love encompasses all people, and God intends that stewardship be practiced for the benefit of the entire human family.

Created in the image of God, persons are together stewards of God's bounty. They are accountable to God for how they use, abuse, or neglect to use the manifold resources—including their own bodies and capacities—which God has placed at their disposal. Reflecting God's cosmic dominion as Creator, they are called to care for the earth and "have dominion over," but not callously dominate, every living thing (Gen. 1:28).

127

Work

Work, the expending of effort for productive ends, is a God-given means by which human creatures exercise dominion. Through work, persons together are enabled to perpetuate life and to enhance its quality. By work they are both privileged and obligated to reflect the Creator whose work they are.

Although sinful rebellion issues in burdens of toil and alienation, the forgiving and renewing Lord holds out the possibility of work as useful and satisfying, prompting the Psalmist's prayer, "Establish the work of our hands" (Ps. 90:17).

Work is thus meant for persons in community, not persons for work. While participation in the community of work is meant to enhance personal well-being, the identity of persons created in God's image is neither defined by the work they do nor destroyed by the absence of work. What a person *does* or *has* does not determine what one *is* as the personal creature of a loving Creator.

Christian identity is also not to be equated with the work Christians do. As new persons in Christ, Christians have been set free and empowered to exercise their vocation through many roles, occupations among them. However, Christians do not equate baptismal vocation in God's kingdom with economic occupations in the world.

Justice

Justice may be described as distributive love. It is what God's love does when many neighbors must be served with limited resources. Justice is the form of God's creating and preserving love as that love is mediated by reason and power through persons and structures in community life. Injustice dehumanizes and prevents full participation in co-humanity. Justice is therefore viewed simply as that which people need to be human.

God mandates the doing of justice (Micah 6:8). The specific content of that justice, however, is not directly revealed but is discovered as life is lived amid claim and counterclaim. The discernment of justice involves every aspect of the human being. It is a task of reason, requiring the counting, measuring and classifying of factors that admit to such analysis. It is intuitive, involving the capacity for empathy. It is political, involving the struggle for power among competing

128

groups. Above all, it is moral, involving the fundamental human capacity to know what enhances and what destroys the being and dignity of the person. That capacity, conscience, grows and is nurtured in the creative interaction of persons and groups, in the recollection of and reflection on past experience, and in the confronting of new situations.

Therefore the doing of justice is the proper stewardship of the social and material resources of creation in which our co-humanity in God's image is being realized.

Social justice refers to those institutional and legal arrangements which promote justice for all the members of society.

In addition to being the way in which God's providential love is expressed socially, justice is also the way in which sinful persons are required to do for others what, in their self-centeredness, they would not otherwise do to meet their neighbors' collective needs.

Because human beings, both individually and collectively, are self-centered, self-serving, and self-justifying, their defining and doing of justice are inevitably tainted by the rationalization of special interest. This sinful rationalization often leads to such errors as the pitting of benevolence against justice and the confusion of justice with righteousness.

Social justice should not be pitted against personal benevolence (often called charity) or corporate benevolence (often called philanthropy); but neither should benevolence be substituted for justice. In its true sense, benevolence is the loving response directly to others in need; in its false sense, it is the vain attempt to purchase a good conscience and to avoid the demand for justice. Rightly understood, benevolence and justice complement each other as different forms of the Creator's providential love.

Neither personal nor corporate benevolence can accomplish what a society is required to do for its members under justice; but a society cannot remain sound if it leaves no room for benevolent acts.

Justice and righteousness, as these terms are used in this statement, are not to be confused or identified with each other. Righteousness denotes the redeeming activity of God in Christ which effects the forgiveness of sin, new life, and salvation. It frees and empowers God's faithful servants to act lovingly and justly in the world, not merely out of prudent self-regard, but also sacrificially for their neighbors' sake.

The attempt to equate human justice and divine righteousness distorts Christ's Gospel and undermines God's law. In the name of liberty, such self-righteousness enslaves; in the name of life, it kills; in the name of abundance, it lays waste. God's holy wrath is provoked when humans presume to rule society by a spurious "gospel," thereby weakening the possibility of realizing justice, peace, and civil order under God's law.

Justice takes place at the intersection of serving love and enlightened self-interest. All sinners, including Christians, are still able as the corrupted image of God to act justly out of such self-regard; and forgiven Christians are empowered to move beyond such self-regard. By the power of Christ working in them, they are freed to enlarge the conventional limits of justice.

While the advancement of justice involves the interplay of countervailing power, it depends finally upon the degree to which the members of a community are either willing or constrained to moderate their acquisitiveness in the interest of the common good.

Justice is a painful process, serving as both the prerequisite for and the fruit of civil peace. Although never fully completed, struggles for justice draw people into the ongoing work of approximating God's will in this sinful world.

Economic Applications

God gives to human creatures the freedom and capacity to devise the means of exercising the stewardship that has been entrusted to them. They may therefore establish such social and legal institutions as will facilitate the life of mutual responsibility for which they have been created. Such humanly-devised means are legitimate so long as they do not usurp the place of God as Lord and owner of all things or thwart the will of God for the well-being of the whole human family.

The Stewardship of Meanings and Values

God enables persons to employ ideas as tools of analysis and evaluation. The fashioning and use of conceptual tools is never finished. New historical situations may require new modes of diagnosis and

130

prescription. The refinement of appropriate concepts is a vital part of the constructive work of seeking justice.

An ideology is a set of linked ideas by which a society, social movement or interest group seeks to explain, give coherence to, and justify a given pattern of behavior or a prescriptive vision for society. An ideology may be used to elicit commitment to preserving the social *status quo* or to changing it.

An ideology can be a useful means for the securing of political cohesion within a society or for mobilizing people in support of constructive change. It can also be used deceptively to mask injustice and to elicit an ultimate commitment which, besides being idolatrous, may make people insensitive to the violation of basic human rights.

No ideology can legitimately be held to be redemptive or represented as embodying God's saving righteousness.

Christians recognize stewardship as including the right use of meanings and values in the just ordering of society and economy. Such ideological stewardship must, however, prevent any system of values from laying an ultimate claim on persons as the bearers of God's image.

As part of the stewardship of meanings and values the following principles are offered as guidance for responsible action.

Government

In a sinful world God intends the institutions of government to be the means of enforcing the claims of economic justice. Government should neither stifle economic freedom through excessive regulation, nor abdicate its responsibility by permitting economic anarchy. Legitimate governmental activity normally includes such functions as protection of workers, producers, and households from practices which are unfair, dangerous, or degrading; protection of the public from deceptive advertising and from dangerous or defective products or processes; encouragement and regulation of public utilities, banking and finance, science and education; environmental protection; provision for the seriously ill and disabled, needy, and unemployed; and establishment of an equitable system of taxation to support these functions. Compliance with these and other legitimate governmental activities should be affirmed, even as their improvement and correction are sought through appropriate political means.

131

In extreme situations, when governmental institutions or holders of political power engage in the tyrannical and systematic violation of basic human rights, and when the means of legal recourse have been exhausted or are demonstrably inadequate, then non-violent direct action, civil disobedience, or, as a last resort, rebellion may become the justifiable and necessary means of establishing those conditions within which justice can again be sought and enjoyed.

Economic Justice

Economic justice is that aspect of social justice involving the material dimension of social relationships and the social activities of production, distribution, and consumption of goods and services. Economic justice denotes the fair apportioning of resources and products, of opportunities and responsibilities, of burdens and benefits among the members of a community. It includes the provision for basic human need, fair compensation for work done, and the opportunity for the full utilization of personal gifts in productive living.

Economic justice includes the elements of equity, accessibility, accountability, and efficiency.

Understood as equity or fairness, economic justice does not mean economic equality. It is rather the result of a discerning of, and response to, the various needs of the members of a society, respecting differences without being partial to power or special interest. Equity implies a sense of the common good and a care for the diversity of gifts and human resources that contribute to it. At the same time it provides for those minimal necessities which, in a given social and cultural setting, are prerequisites for participation in society; and it provides for those members of the society who, because of circumstances not of their making, cannot provide for themselves.

Accessibility includes both the formal entitlements to political participation and legal redress, and such substantive entitlements (e.g., nutrition, shelter, health care, basic education, minimum income and/ or employment) as are needed for entrance into the social and economic community. It also includes the provision of the means by which the members of a community may participate in decisions which affect the quality of the common life and that of future generations.

Accountability implies that economic actors must be held answerable to the community for the consequences of their behavior. Government properly establishes the legal means whereby people may secure compensation for injury incurred, as a result of economic decisions which have not taken account of their likely impact on personal and community well-being.

Efficiency requires a responsible use of resources that is genuinely productive by minimizing waste. This productivity is conserving not only of material resources and time, but also of human resources and the environment. The economy should be structured to permit the calculation of efficiency so as to take account of social and ecological waste.

Persons should be permitted and encouraged to participate in fundamental as well as market decisions governing the economy. Members of a society should be co-determiners of the quality of their economic life. Such co-determination, requiring differing structures appropriate for differing situations, is the basic right of persons whom God has created in co-humanity as responsible stewards.

Stewardship requires careful forethought. Planning is vital to the stewardship of material resources at all levels of human life: personal, familial, communal, and political. Planning on economic matters is more than technical. Questions of basic human value are involved in both specifying economic goals and devising the means of achieving them.

Planning should therefore be sufficiently pluralistic in character to assure the possibility of self-correction and prevent domination by one or a few special interests. It should be done on a scale and level of social life which will provide the greatest practical degree of participation and co-determination.

God has implanted in the human creature the capacity and initiative to define the problems of material existence in community and to effect positive change. No person or community should relinquish that initiative or capacity, and social and political institutions should be designed to encourage such initiative at the local and intermediate levels of society. A society is healthier when its members are encouraged to participate responsibly in determining their own lives rather than being only the passive consumers of goods and services.

Work

Even in the present state of sinful estrangement, God's intention remains that work be done and its fruits be enjoyed by the whole human family. The division of labor according to efficiency and the diversity of human gifts, along with the social relations of productive activity, are means by which life in co-humanity may be both extended and enriched.

Work that is beneficial to society glorifies the Creator. Those who perform such work are to be esteemed for their contribution to the common good. They are not to be judged by whether or not the work is remunerative, or by the amount of remuneration. Vast disparities of income and wealth are both divisive of the human community and demeaning to its members.

Exclusion of persons from the community of work is a denial of the opportunity of realizing the divine intention for co-humanity.

Humanly-devised economic arrangements which, in their operation, tend both to exclude some persons from the community of work, and subsequently to stigmatize such persons for not working, constitute a double affront to the Creator and to persons created in God's image.

Property

The concept of property is a legal means of determining responsibility for the use of resources and humanly-produced wealth. Property may be held by individuals, by business corporations, by cooperative or communal self-help organizations, or by government. In whatever manner it is held, property is held in trust and its holder is accountable ultimately to God and proximately to the community through its constituted authorities for the ways in which the resource or wealth is, or is not, used.

While the holder of wealth-producing property is entitled to a reasonable return, as determined contextually by the society, the holder of such property may not assert exclusive claim on it or its fruits. Justice requires that wealth be both productive and contributory to the general well-being through both the provision of new opportunities and the alleviation of human need.

The private ownership of property is a humanly devised legal right which can serve as a means for the exercise of that responsible stewardship which constitutes the divine image. Private property is not an absolute human right but is always conditioned by the will of God and the needs of the community. The obligation to serve justifies the right to possess. The Creator does not sanction the accumulation of economic power and possessions as ends in themselves.

Conclusion

We affirm the inseparability of the economy from the whole of human life. The criticism and reshaping of economic relations and institutions is a fundamentally moral task in which Christians should be actively involved. Economy, rightly understood, is the God-given stewardship of life.

In Christ the People of God are freed and enabled individually and corporately to participate in the quest for greater economic justice and the achievement of the conditions of human well-being. As a worldwide community of brothers and sisters, the church can summon the human family to care for the earth responsibly while God yet gives us time.

Implementing Resolution

This church calls upon its ministers and congregations to engage in an intensive study over the next biennium of the social statement, "Economic Justice: Stewardship of Creation in Human Community," with a view to ascertaining the content of this church's corporate stewardship within the present historical setting. Such study is to consider both the institutional allocation of the material and human resources of this church internally and the work of public advocacy by this church externally.

This church directs its program agencies and offices to facilitate such study through programs appropriate to their several mandates. Such work should to the extent possible be planned and executed through such means as the Staff Team on World Hunger Concerns and the Staff Team on Fiscal Support. Each churchwide agency shall report to the 1982 convention of this church the results of its study and action, as well as its future intentions in the field of economic justice.

Efforts are to be made by appropriate agencies of this church to equip both the ministers and the laity to understand and apply the orientation and principles embodied in this statement through such means as:

1) Seminary and college curricula;

2) Continuing education for pastors;

3) Conferences for parish lay leadership;

4) Church school curricula; and

5) Faith and Life Institutes.

The Division for Mission in North America shall advise this church as to appropriate ways of implementing this statement both through advocacy in the public sector and through consultation and shareholder action in the private corporate sector.

The administrative offices of this church, in consultation with the Division for Mission in North America, shall study this statement with a view to the application of its principles to this church as a manager of resources, employer, fund-raiser, investor, and purchaser and provider of goods and services.

The Division for Mission in North America shall continue the work of issue-clarification and the constructive criticism of ideology begun during the preparation of this statement. It shall continue to involve the lay persons of relevant expertise and experience who were engaged in the development of this statement as well as others whom it may identify.

The Division for Mission in North America, through its program, Advocacy for Global Justice, shall identify and act upon the global and domestic implications of this statement as they impinge on the reality of world hunger.

This church shall endeavor to implement this statement through its inter-Lutheran and ecumenical involvements, both in North America and worldwide.

A Statement by Lutheran World Relief

Toward the Development of a United States Food Policy

Endorsed by the Seventh Biennial Convention
Lutheran Church in America
1974

The Background of Our Involvement

For nearly three decades, Lutheran World Relief has been committed to assist in alleviating human suffering stemming from war, disaster, social upheaval, famine, and endemic need. Lutheran World Relief has supported programs in 56 countries, utilizing food, medicine, clothing, equipment and cash—with a total value in excess of $300 million. More than half of this was provided through voluntary contributions in cash and kind from individual U.S. Lutherans as well as their national organizations, The American Lutheran Church, the Lutheran Church in America, and The Lutheran Church—Missouri Synod. The remainder consisted of gifts of food and fiber from the United States Government and cash reimbursements of ocean freight by the United States and foreign governments.

Through current activities in thirty countries on three continents, Lutheran World Relief has an opportunity to view at close range the intense suffering of poor people and poor nations of the world. Our distinctive motivation as Christian Churches enforces our desire to cooperate with other organizations and with our Government in responding to pressing human needs. Against this background of involvement and concern, the Board of Directors of Lutheran World Relief has approved the following statement:

The Basis of Our Urgent Concern

Lutheran World Relief feels compelled to express its conviction regarding the need for new policies and enlarged programs under which the United States will increase its efforts to meet the needs of hungry and starving persons. At the heart of our concern is the very real possibility that death from starvation may strike down more people in a single year than were killed in World Wars I and II. Equally tragic is the likelihood that each year more than a million children will suffer severe and permanent brain damage for lack of proper food. Their impairment will burden their families and their nations. It ought also to burden the consciences of affluent people and nations throughout the world.

Specific factors which prompt us to register our concern include the following:

The dangerous dwindling of the world's food reserve;

The warning of meteorologists that the United States may experience a severe drought within the next five years similar to those of the 1930s and 1950s, which would work hardship on our own citizens but would result in starvation for millions of persons in other nations who are heavily dependent upon our exportable food supply to meet their needs;

The small but significant change in the world's climate which threatens to make crippling drought a regular occurrence for some parts of the world while bringing excessively high and destructive levels of rainfall to other parts;

The unceasing trend toward increased consumption of food (especially animal protein), fuel and other resources by affluent people and nations without regard for the resultant consequences to poor nations and people;

The prospect that affluent nations which can "pay the price" may corner the market on food, fuel and fertilizer, leaving poorer nations and people to face starvation;

The recent decline in the availability of food under the Food for Peace program of the United States Government.

The United Nations, in its Universal Declaration of Human Rights, declared on behalf of every human being "the right to food." Yet 25 years after the passage of this declaration this basic right seems frequently to be regarded as an option which may or may not be granted, depending upon economic, political or other factors which may intervene. We reject the idea that "compassion fatigue" from years of overseas assistance should now determine the response of the United States towards the world's poor. The United States, as the greatest consumer-producer nation in the world, must exercise leadership and direct its great strength and resources towards the solution of these massive human problems. Failure to take decisive action would constitute an erosion of the humanity of this nation and its people.

Proposals for Positive Action

We call for prompt action by the United States Government which will mitigate the ravages of hunger and the concurrent disabling effects it brings upon nations and people enslaved by it. We further urge action which will initiate efforts of preparedness against unforeseen but predictable contingencies which could deprive millions of poor people of food sufficient to support life.

To that end we encourage the adoption now of new policies which will clearly demonstrate the positive commitment of the United States to the hungry people of the world. These policies should:

1. Commit annually at least 10% of food grains available for support for use in programs of humanitarian assistance through intergovernmental, governmental and voluntary agencies to assist endangered children, aging and infirm persons and victims of disaster as well as facilitate human development through self-help;

2. Assure the use of food so designated on the basis of need and without discrimination as to the ethnic origin or political persuasion of the recipients, in order that food not be used as a political tool;

3. Encourage maximum agricultural production in the United States to provide greater assistance in meeting the world's increasing need for food;

4. Establish multi-year (instead of annual) commitments with voluntary agency partners in order to enhance the possibility of sound planning for program development;

5. Give leadership and support for the development of an international network of national food reserves under coordination of the Food and Agriculture Organization of the United Nations to meet emergency needs resulting from crop failures or other disasters;

6. Increase support for the United Nations Children's Emergency Fund (UNICEF), the Food and Agriculture Organization (FAO), and the World Food Program (WFP) as a means of enlisting the cooperation of the world community in meeting essential needs of the whole human family;

7. Establish safeguards against extreme fluctuation of agricultural commodity prices which, in view of full production and development of national food reserves, might place disproportionate responsibility and risk upon the American farmer;

8. Enlist the support of other affluent nations in providing assistance to the poor of all nations;

9. Encourage citizen initiatives in reducing wasteful and excessive use of food, fuel and fertilizer;

10. Provide for the establishment of economic relations and mechanisms which will achieve more effective production and more equitable distribution of food;

11. Support and stimulate research for discovering and developing new food resources and for increased food production through husbandry of the sea.

Other Essential Considerations

While the foregoing emphasizes the need to establish new policies for the use of food, we also wish to register our conviction that simultaneous and urgent efforts must be directed in other avenues as well. Both government and voluntary agencies must intensify their efforts to enhance agricultural production and social and economic development in poor nations as well as to deal with the problems of energy availability and population growth. Toward each of these areas we believe this nation should continue to provide leadership and should increase its commitment of resources.

Notes

Preface

1. *Minutes,* Ninth Biennial Convention of the Lutheran Church in America, July 12-19, 1978, p. 362.
2. *Minutes,* Seventh Biennial Convention of the Lutheran Church in America, July 3-10, 1974, p. 726.
3. Ibid.
4. Ibid., pp. 739-42.
5. Ibid., p. 42.
6. Ibid., pp. 699-70, 725.
7. *Social Statements,* Lutheran Church in America, Division for Mission in North America, 231 Madison Avenue, New York, New York 10016.
8. Commission on Church and State Relations in a Pluralistic Society, *Church and State: A Lutheran Perspective* (New York: Lutheran Church in America) 1963.

Introduction

1. William S. Vickrey, "An Exchange of Questions between Economics and Philosophy," *Goals of Economic Life,* ed. A.D. Ward (New York: Harper 1953) p. 56.

Chapter 1

1. Richard Burt, "U.S. Curbs Technology for Soviet," *New York Times,* 19 March 1980, pp. D1, 13. It has been suggested that the U.S. embargo of oil-extraction technology to the Soviet Union may contribute to an outcome opposite to the one intended. The development of its domestic reserves being thwarted by the U.S. embargo, the USSR will become more dependent on Middle East resources and, thereby, be tempted to further "adventurism." See Marshall I. Goldman, "The Soviet Oil Alarm," *New York Times,* 17 April 1980, p. A27.

2. Richard J. Barnett, "The World's Resources: 1. The Lean Years," A Reporter at Large, *New Yorker,* 17 March 1980, p. 54.

3. Ibid.

Chapter 2

1. Adam Smith, *The Wealth of Nations* (New York: Random House, 1957), p. 743. See also Howard Richards, "Adam Smith, Milton Friedman and Christian Economics," *The Earth is the Lord's*, ed. Mary Evelyn Jegan and Bruno V. Manno (New York: Paulist Press, 1978).

   Smith took a dim view of the moral teaching and preaching of "the little sects" which he saw as potentially disruptive, "unsocial," and "disagreeably rigorous." He thought such dissonant moralizing could be effectively countered by liberal education for the upper classes and "the frequency and gaiety of public diversions" for the masses. He would probably have approved of television and the Super Bowl!

2. Contrasting evaluations of the diverse thought of Smith, particularly in regard to his value theory, are those of such neoclassicists as Paul C. Douglas in *Adam Smith, 1776-1926* (Chicago: University of Chicago Press, 1928), or such Marxists as Maurice Dobb in *Political Economy and Capitalism* (Westport, Connecticut: Greenwood, 1945) and Ronald L. Meek, *Studies in the Labor Theory of Value* (New York: Monthly Review Press, 1956). All of these illustrate how the thought of Smith gave rise to widely divergent ideological positions. At the same time, each sees in Smith the seeds of a "scientifically objective economics." Dobb goes so far as to celebrate Smith as the economic equivalent of Newton, likening the labor theory of value to the law of gravity.

3. Friedrich A. Hayek, *The Mirage of Social Justice,* Law, Legislation and Liberty, vol. 2 (Chicago: The University of Chicago Press, 1978). Hayek actually treats economic or distributive justice as synonymous with social justice and, therefore, as equally devoid of meaning. See, for instance, p. 7.

4. Milton Friedman and Rose Friedman, *Freedom to Choose* (New York: Harcourt Brace Jovanovich, 1980), and *Capitalism and Freedom* (Chicago: University of Chicago Press, 1962).

142

5. Adam Smith, *The Theory of Moral Sentiments* (London: Henry C. Bohn, 1961), p. 117. Smith's contention that such misplaced concern can be bad for business and, therefore, the economic system is echoed today by Milton Friedman. See Howard Richards, "Adam Smith, Milton Friedman and Christian Economics," *The Earth is the Lord's*, ed. Jegan and Manno, p. 56.

6. Hayek, op. cit., p. 66. See also Edward Norman, *Church and Society in England, 1170-1970: A Historical Study* (Oxford: Clarendon Press, 1976). Norman's and Hayek's representation of the Christian faith as individualist and spiritualist is coming into vogue in reaction to the activist "corporate moralism" to be discussed in chapter 3. However, their understanding of Christian faith is totally erroneous.

7. See, inter alia, Waldo Beach and H. Richard Niebuhr, eds., *Christian Ethics: Sources of the Living Tradition* (New York: Roland Press, 1955); George W. Forell, ed., *Christian Social Teachings* (Garden City, New York: Doubleday, 1966). And, since Hayek is particularly pointed in his criticism of Roman Catholic thought, see John C. Haughey, ed., *The Faith that Does Justice* (New York: Woodstock Theological Center, 1977).

8. See Howard Richards and Juan Metz Lopehandia, "Economic Justice: Appraisal of Quito Declaration," Alternative II (North Holland Publishing Company, 1976), pp. 61-69.

9. One country that appears thus far to have withstood the trend toward food dependency is Malawi. See Pranay B. Gupte, "Corn is Green in Thriving Malawi, but Dark Clouds Loom," *New York Times,* 27 February 1980.

10. The Structural-Functionalist school of sociological theory early sought to devise categories of social development that could be applied irrespective of culture and history. Consult works by Verba and Almond as listed in bibliography.

11. The force of criticism has led to a general reappraisal of the viability of a "scientific" approach to modernization and development. While scholars have responded to this chastening in a variety of ways, they may for convenience be classified into the following groups:

a. The committed liberal theorists who, while retaining and refining the theories of modernization, are more candid than earlier theorists about their normative or ideological commitments;

b. Those who have abandoned the quest for a comprehensive theory of modernization, opting instead for the analysis of smaller chunks of reality;

c. Those who, having severely criticized modernization theory, would now substitute another comprehensive approach, usually some version of Marxist theory.

It should be emphasized in passing that while the new theoretical style involves a certain ideological candor whatever the scholar's normative biases, there remains a (salutory) concern for the maintenance of scientific rigor in the selection and arrangement of data so as to provide a degree of objectivity and, therefore, credibility to the presentation. The requirements of clarity, theoretical consistency and accuracy in the empirical measurements continue to be recognized and generally respected.

Rejecting as they do the concept of value-free analysis, Marxist scholars look upon modernization theory and the norms embedded in it as a reflection of the Western political economic situation and the relation of dominance-dependence that exists between the West and the countries of the Third World.

Having delivered some of the most trenchant criticism of the ethnocentrism, generality and timelessness characteristic of modernization theory, serious scholars of a Marxist orientation are hard put not to repeat the errors. Many acknowledge the pitfall of Eurocentricity in a too rigid application of Marxist categories to the lived reality of the Third World.

12. The so-called battlefield on lifeboat ethic. Those whose chances of survival are slim are permitted to perish in order not to deplete the resources needed by those better off. The debate raged in the early 1970s. See, for instance, the writings of Garrett Hardin.

13. See Bonnie Campbell, "Ivory Coast," *West African States: Failure and Promise,* ed. John Dunn (Cambridge: Cambridge University Press, 1978).

14. As discussed by Martti Lindqvist in *Economic Growth and the Quality of Life* (Helsinki: Finnish Society for Missiology and Ecumenics, 1975), pp. 8-66.

Chapter 3

1. Joan Didion, *The White Album* (New York: Simon and Schuster, 1978), p. 93.

2. Ibid.

3. John Updike, *The Coup* (New York: Fawcett Crest, 1978), pp. 50, 51.

4. Reinhold Niebuhr, *Moral Man and Immoral Society* (New York: Charles Scribner's Sons, 1932), pp. 113-41.

5. Didion, op. cit., p. 89.

6. "It's Our Planet—It's Our Hunger Project," Publication of EST-Related Hunger Project, San Francisco, California, p. 5. See, also, David Hoekema, "The Hunger Project: You Can't Eat Words," *Christian Century*, 2 May 1979, pp. 486-7.

7. See, inter alia, Robert M. Price, "A Fundamentalist Social Gospel?" *Christian Century*, 28 November 1979, pp. 1183-6.

8. William Vickrey, "Economic Rationality and Social Choice," *Social Research* 44, no. 4 (Winter 1977): 647.

9. K.H. Ting (Ding Kuangumn), "A Sermon by K.H. Ting," *Information Letter: Marxism and China Study* (Geneva: Lutheran World Federation, October 1979), p. 18.

10. Ibid., p. 19.

11. The European origin of many of the concepts informing liberation theology (in the writings of such persons as Metz, Bloch, Golwitzer and Moltmann) is well known; and the dissemination of these ideas by expatriate religious, often members of missionary orders, is equally evident. That much of the "revolutionary reflection" and publication emanates from such places of privilege as Westchester County, New York, while not invalidating it, does suggest that there is a much more complicated linkage between the communities of privilege and of poverty than that suggested by the usual rhetoric of liberation theology.

12. Youssel M. Ibrahim, "Inside Iran's Cultural Revolution," *New York Times Magazine*, 14 October 1978, p. 78.

13. See Jose Miguez Bonino, "Church, People and the Avant-Garde," *Doing Theology in a Revolutionary Situation* (Philadelphia: Fortress Press, 1975), pp. 154-74.

14. Reinhold Niebuhr, op. cit., pp. 142-99.

Chapter 4

1. A classic articulation of the communal/historical context of the hermeneutical task is H. Richard Niebuhr's *The Meaning of Revelation* (New York: Macmillan, 1960). Christian hermeneutics can only be done within the circle of faith and in the light of the believing community's experience of and response to God's action in Christ. "When the church speaks of revelation it never means simply the Scriptures, but only the Scriptures read from the point of view and in the context of Church history" (p. 50).

   More recently Hans Küng has addressed the same issue. For him, Christian hermeneutics is done in the context of space/time amid a pluralism of voices. Within such a context, the truly "Catholic theologian" will always start out from the fact that there was never a time when the Gospel was left without witness and he will try to learn from the church of the past. While insisting on the necessity of critical scrutiny, he will never overlook the boundary posts and danger signals which the church in former times, in its concern and struggle for the one true faith, often at times of great distress and danger, set up in the form of creeds and definitions to distinguish between good and bad interpretations of the message. He will never neglect the positive and negative experiences of his fathers and brothers in theology, those teachers who are his older and more experienced fellow students in the school of sacred Scripture. It is precisely in this critical scrutiny that the Catholic theologian is interested in the *continuity* which is preserved through the disruptions.

   "The Catholic theologian will always start out from the fact that the Gospel has not left itself without witness to any nation, any class or race, and he will try to learn from other churches. However deeply rooted he may be in a particular local church, he will not tie his theology to a particular nation, culture, race, class, form of society, ideology or school. Precisely in his specific loyalty, the Catholic theologian is interested in the *universality* of the Christian faith embracing all groups." Hans Küng, "Why I Remain a Catholic," *New York Times,* 28 January 1980, p. A17.

2. This orientation is classically set forth in Luther's *Treatise on Christian Liberty.* It has received explication, inter alia, in George W. Forell, *Faith Active in Love* (New York: American Press,

1954) and Paul Ramsey, *Basic Christian Ethics* (New York: Charles Scribner's Sons, 1950). In the latter see, esp., pp. 133-52.

3. See Foster R. McCurley and John H. Reumann, "The Sheep and the Goats," (concluding section of "Historical Disasters and the Final Judgment") *Population Perils,* ed. George W. Forell and William H. Lazareth, Justice Books (Philadelphia: Fortress Press, 1979), pp. 26-31. See, also, A.J. Mattill Jr., "What the World Owes the Church," *Homiletical and Pastoral Review* 71 (1971): 8-17; and, by the same author, "Matthew 25:31-46 Relocated," *Restoration Quarterly* 17 (1974): 107-14.

4. Not only party strife but class division seems to have plagued the early church, causing disharmony even in the Lord's Supper itself. Paul takes to task the Corinthian congregation for allowing divisions between "haves" and "have nots" to rend the Body of Christ and making the eucharistic meal into an eating and drinking of condemnation (1 Cor. 11:17-22).

Blatant class division also characterized the congregations to which the general letter of James was addressed. It is unfortunate and not a little distressing that James' voice is muted in the lectionary of the *Lutheran Book of Worship.* In Lectionary B, the second lesson appointed for the Seventeenth Sunday after Pentecost is listed as James 2:1-5, 8-10, 14-18. By omitting verses 6 and 7, the reading is so softened as to lose its prophetic ring: "But you have dishonored the poor man. Is it not the rich who oppress you, is it not they who drag you into court? Is it not they who blaspheme that honorable name by which you are called?" Such treatment of the passage deprives today's faithful of the reminder that in the present age the church also bears the evidence of injustice. There are segments of the world-wide church whose relation to the poor merits the description given by James to the churches of his time. See *Lutheran Book of Worship,* prepared by the churches participating in the Inter-Lutheran Commission on Worship (Minneapolis/Philadelphia: Augsburg Publishing House, Board of Publication, LCA, 1979), p. 27.

5. Of the standard readings *The Interpreter's Bible* is typical. Sherman E. Johnson in the exegesis designates the passage a "parable" which reflects the "ethical spirit" of the Old Testament

"eloquently and beautifully" expressing "the heart of religion" as understood by the Jewish Christian congregation. And in the exposition George Buttrick identifies "all the nations" as including both Gentiles and Jews who knew but rejected Jesus and his identification with the poor. Judgment is pronounced on anyone who neglected "a brother man indwelt by Christ." *The Interpreter's Bible,* vol. 7 (New York: Abingdon Press, 1951) pp. 562-3, 566.

6. Hymn 424, *Lutheran Book of Worship.*

7. Theodore G. Tappert, ed. and trans., *The Book of Concord* (Philadelphia: Fortress Press, 1959), p. 391.

8. Ibid., p. 164.

9. Martin Luther, "The Sermon on the Mount," *Luther's Works,* ed. Jaroslav Pelikan (St. Louis: Concordia, 1956), p. 30.

10. Roland Bainton, ed. and trans. *The Martin Luther Christmas Book* (Philadelphia: Muhlenberg, 1958), p. 65.

11. Helmut Thielicke, *Theological Ethics,* vol. 1, trans. William H. Lazareth (Philadelphia: Fortress Press, 1960), p. 303.

12. Ibid., p. 70.

13. Ibid., p. 303; cf. pp. 20, 21.

14. Gustavo Gutierrez, *A Theology of Liberation* (Maryknoll, New York: Orbis Books, 1973), p. 197 and footnotes, esp. 24 and 26, p. 210.

15. Ibid., p. 170.

16. Ibid., p. 200: Gutierrez reads Matthew's Last Judgment as dealing with "human mediation to reach God." "[L]ove for God is unavoidably expressed through love of one's neighbor . . . God is love in the neighbor . . . To love one's brother . . . *is* to love God: 'You did it for me . . . you did it not for me'" cf. pp. 198ff.; p. 201. "[W]e find God in our encounters with men, especially the poor . . . an act of love towards them is an act of love towards God."

17. Ibid., p. 202: "[E]veryman is a lottery vendor who offers us 'the big one': our encounter with that God who is deep down in the heart of each man." It is understandable, but nevertheless puzzling, to see how metaphors from an essentially feudal political

economy persist in the thought of the liberationists. The lottery image is a striking example; and the insistence that the poor are the means to communion with God is straight out of the medieval context.

18. Notwithstanding his opting for the "conventional" reading of Matthew, Gutierrez elsewhere appears to identify the oppressed with the Elect of God, suggesting that the Elect are sometimes anonymous and unaware of their election. Cf. pp. 151 and 228. This theme is expanded on at length by Jose Miguez Bonino in *Doing Theology in a Revolutionary Situation,* esp. pp. 154, 173.

Chapter 5

1. Martin Luther, "The Small Catechism," *The Book of Concord,* ed. and trans. Theodore G. Tappert, p. 345.

2. Paul (and the mainstream of classical Christianity) rejected the Greek denial of the material world and the relegation of sexual reproduction and the home to the realm of "mere matter" (hyle). The picture of a heroic Socrates, dismissing his wife Xantippe and their children for the preferred fellowship of intellectual love, is most assuredly not a paradigm for Christians. See Plato, *The Phaedo,* trans. Benjamin Jowett (New York: Random House, 1928), p. 622.

   The Hellenistic ethos, as manifested in such forms as Neoplatonism, Gnosticism and Stoicism held the body, the passions and the world of change and death to be of little account. Sexuality was considered not a part of "essential" being, but a mark of deficiency, of non-being. True "being" in the realm of the ideal was considered to be asexual, impassive and unchanging. The task of the soul was to escape the body by transcending all that partakes of non-being: matter, passion and change. It was required to pass from the hylic through the psychic to the pneumatic level of being.

   As part of the hylic, sexuality was to be overcome through contemplation and the mortification of the flesh. This originally neoplatonic orientation is still a problem for the church as it seeks to relate to the world.

The devaluation of the body leads both to the denial and the abuse of sex. Ascetism and debauchery are actually two sides of a single coin. So Aldous Huxley in *Brave New World* rightly depicts the "pneumatic" elite as, at one and the same time, viewing sexual reproduction as disgustingly dirty, and sexual promiscuity as not only a right but a duty. Refusal to affirm the pleasure principle is tantamount to treason against the perfect society.

The Christian witness maintains that sexuality, far from being a mark of deficiency, is essential to—indeed, constitutive of—the co-humanity by which God is imaged. The heterosexual difference (and, therefore, mutual need and interdependence) is God's good gift to the human family. Sexuality and sex are not the evidence of an "existential defect." Sin, the refusal to trust God and obey him, manifests itself in the despising of sexuality, through abuse and/or denial, and the sundering of co-humanity.

3. Richard H. Luecke, "Unemployment and the Future of Work," *Work as Praise,* Justice Books, ed. George W. Forell and William H. Lazareth (Philadelphia: Fortress Press, 1979), pp. 7-15.

4. Quoted by Ron Nessen in "Political Wisecracks: Some Front-Runners," *New York Times,* 5 December 1979, p. C11.

5. Reinhold Niebuhr, *Moral Man and Immoral Society,* pp. 113-141.

6. "Aging and the Older Adult," Social Statements of the Lutheran Church in America, 1978.

7. Hannah Arendt, *The Human Condition* (Chicago: University of Chicago Press, 1958), p. 114.

8. Ibid., p. 115.

9. Tappert, *Book of Concord,* p. 290.

10. Hayek, *The Mirage of Social Justice,* p. 74: "[A] belief in a . . . moral justification of individual success . . . in the Anglo-Saxon world . . . received strong support from Calvinist teaching."

11. Forell, *Christian Social Teachings,* p. 279.

12. See, for instance, "John Wesley and the Laity: An Interview with Albert C. Outler," The Audenshaw Foundation, Doc. 1619, 1979.

13. Forell, *Christian Social Teachings,* p. 283.

14. Waldo Beach and H. Richard Niebuhr point out that Wesley himself directed his words to people of modest means. Yet the frugality of these people was the means of their embourgeoisement. *Christian Ethics: Sources of the Living Tradition* (New York: Roland Press, 1955), pp. 361-65.

15. Tappert, *Book of Concord,* p. 430.

16. On "the possible effectiveness of private property," William Vickrey makes the following observations: "There remains, however, the possibility that future developments may rob the individual of the fruits of his abstention and foresight in a way that does not entirely destroy their value to society. The individual who postponed exploitation of his resources runs the risk of expropriation, onerous taxation or private depredation. Political instability is thus inimical to conservation, or at least to conservation through the institution of private property. Excessive political stability on the other hand is inimical to progress and to many important values. At this point, an extremely wide range of values conflict." *Goals of Economic Life,* p. 53. See, also, Vickrey, "An Economist's View of Human Rights," *Small Comfort in Hard Times,* ed. Michael Mooney and Florian Stuber (New York: Columbia University Press, 1977).

17. See Franklin D. Fry, *Justice* (Philadelphia: Parish Life Press, 1978), p. 66.

18. See Howard Richards, *The Earth is the Lord's*, p. 53.

19. Tappert, *Book of Concord,* pp. 498ff., 634-5.

20. Steven Erlanger, "Iran's Shaky Theocracy. Khomeini: The God that Failed," *New Republic,* 10 November 1978, pp. 12,14.

21. See, for instance, Theodore N. Schultz, *Investment in Human Capital* (New York: Free Press, 1970).

Chapter 6

1. Luecke, "Unemployment and the Future of Work," *Work as Praise,* pp. 7,8.

2. Peter L. Berger and Richard J. Neuhaus, *To Empower People: The Role of Mediating Structures in Public Policy* (Washington,

D.C.: American Enterprise Institute for Public Policy Research, 1977).

3. Christopher Lasch, *The Culture of Narcissm: American Life in an Age of Diminishing Expectations* (New York: Warner Books, 1979).

4. Gudina Tumsa, "The Role of a Christian in a Given Society," *Lutheran World Information,* 13 February 1980, p. 18.

BIBLIOGRAPHY

Almond, Gabriel A. *Crisis, Choice and Change*. Boston: Little, Brown, 1973.

Almond, Gabriel A., and Coleman, James S., eds. *The Politics of Developing Areas*. Princeton: Princeton University Press, 1960.

Almond, Gabriel A., and Powell, G. Bingham. *Comparative Politics: A Developmental Approach*. Boston: Little, Brown, 1966.

Almond, Gabriel A., and Verba, Sidney. *The Civic Culture*. Princeton University Press, 1963.

Apter, David E. *Choice and the Points of Allocation: A Developmental Theory*. New Haven: Yale University Press, 1971.

Archer, Angus. *Scanning Our Future: A Report from the NGO Forum on the World Economic Order*. New York: Carnegie Endowment for International Peace, 1975.

Arendt, Hannah. *The Human Condition*. Chicago: University of Chicago Press, 1958.

Bainton, Roland, ed. and trans. *The Martin Luther Christmas Book*. Philadelphia: Muhlenberg, 1958.

Barnett, Richard J. "The World's Resources: 1. The Lean Years." A Reporter at Large. *New Yorker,* 17 March 1980, p. 54.

Beach, Waldo, and Niebuhr, H. Richard, eds. *Christian Ethics: Sources of the Living Tradition*. New York: Roland Press, 1955.

Berger, Peter L. *Pyramids of Sacrifice: Political Ethics and Social Change*. New York: Basic Books, 1974.

Berger, Peter L., and Neuhaus, Richard J. *To Empower People: The Role of Mediating Structures in Public Policy*. Washington, D.C.: American Enterprise Institute for Public Policy Research, 1977.

Bonino, Jose Miguez. *Doing Theology in a Revolutionary Situation*. Edited by William H. Lazareth. Philadelphia: Fortress Press, 1975.

Burt, Richard. "U.S. Curbs Technology for Soviet." *New York Times,* 19 March 1980, pp. D1,13.

Claude, Richard P. *Comparative Human Rights.* Baltimore: Johns Hopkins, 1976.

Commission on Church and State Relations in a Pluralistic Society. *Church and State: A Lutheran Perspective.* New York: Lutheran Church in America, 1963.

Committee for Economic Development. *Improving Productivity in State and Local Government.* Washington, D.C.: CED, 1976.

Committee on Economic Development. *Redefining Government's Role in the Market System.* Washington, D.C.: CED, 1979.

Commoner, Barry. *The Poverty of Power: Energy and the Economic Crisis.* New York: Knopf, 1976.

Decke, Gerd, ed. *The Encounter of the Church with Movements of Social Change in Various Cultural Contexts.* Geneva: Lutheran World Federation, 1977.

Didion, Joan. *The White Album.* New York: Simon and Schuster, 1978.

Dunn, John. *West African States: Failure and Promise.* Cambridge: Cambridge University Press, 1978.

Eckholm, Erik. *The Dispossessed of the Earth: Land Reform and Sustainable Development.* Washington, D.C.: Worldwatch Institute, 1979.

Erlich, Paul R., and Feldman, S. Shirley. *The Race Bomb.* New York: Ballantine Books, 1977.

Fairlie, Henry. *The Seven Deadly Sins Today.* Washington, D.C.: New Republic Books, 1978.

Forell, George W., ed. *Christian Social Teachings.* Garden City, New York: Doubleday, 1966.

Forell, George W., and Lazareth, William H., eds. *Population Perils.* Justice Books. Philadelphia: Fortress Press, 1979.

Forell, George W., and Lazareth, William H., eds. *Work as Praise.* Justice Books. Philadelphia: Fortress Press, 1979.

Friedman, Milton, and Friedman, Rose D. *Capitalism and Freedom.* Chicago: University of Chicago Press, 1962.

154

Friedman, Milton, and Friedman, Rose D. *Freedom to Choose: A Personal Statement*. New York: Harcourt Brace Jovanovich, 1980.

Fry, Franklin D. *Justice*. Philadelphia: Parish Life Press, 1978.

Galbraith, John Kenneth. *Economics and the Public Purpose*. Boston: Houghton Mifflin, 1973.

Goulet, Denis. *The Cruel Choice: A New Concept in the Theory of Development*. New York: Atheneum, 1975.

Goulet, Denis. *The Uncertain Promise: Value Conflicts in Technology Transfer*. New York: IDOC North America, 1977.

Gunnemann, Jon P. *The Nation-State and Transnational Corporations in Conflict with Special Reference to Latin America*. New York: Praeger, 1975.

Gutierrez, Gustavo. *A Theology of Liberation*. Maryknoll, New York: Orbis Books, 1973.

Gutkind, Peter C.W., and Wallerstein, Immanuel. *The Political Economy of Contemporary Africa*. Beverly Hills/London: Sage, 1976.

Hardin, Garrett J. *Exploring New Ethics for Survival: The Voyage of the Spaceship Beagle*. New York: Viking Press, 1972.

Hardin, Garrett J. *The Limits of Altruism: An Ecologist's View of Survival*. Bloomington: Indiana University Press, 1977.

Haughey, John C., ed. *The Faith that does Justice*. New York: Woodstock Theological Center, 1977.

Hayek, Friedrich A. *The Mirage of Social Justice*. Law, Legislation and Liberty, vol. 2. Chicago: University of Chicago Press, 1974.

Hayek, Friedrich A. *The Road to Serfdom*. Chicago: University of Chicago Press, 1944.

Heilbroner, Robert L. *An Inquiry into the Human Prospect*. New York: W.W. Norton, 1974.

Heilbroner, Robert L. *Between Capitalism and Socialism: Essays in Political Economics*. New York: Vintage Books, 1970.

Heilbroner, Robert L. *Marxism: For and Against*. New York: W.W. Norton, 1980.

Hessel, Dieter T., ed. *Energy Ethics*. New York: Friendship Press, 1979.

Huxley, Aldous. *Brave New World Revisited*. New York: Harper and Row, 1959.

The Interpreter's Bible, vol. 7. New York: Abingdon Press, 1951.

Jackson, Richard A., ed. *The Multinational Corporation and Social Policy: Special Reference to General Motors in South Africa*. New York: Praeger, 1974.

Jegen, Mary Evelyn, and Manno, Bruno V. *The Earth is the Lord's*. New York: Paulist Press, 1978.

Lasch, Christopher. *The Culture of Narcissism: American Life in an Age of Diminishing Expectations*. New York: Warner Books, 1979.

Lazareth, William H., ed. *The Left Hand of God: Essays on Discipleship and Patriotism*. Philadelphia: Fortress Press, 1976.

Lekachman, Robert. *Economists at Bay: Why the Experts Will Never Solve Your Problems*. New York: McGraw Hill, 1976.

Leontief, Wassily. *The Future of the World Economy: A United Nations Study.* New York: Oxford University Press, 1977.

Lindbeck, Assar. *The Political Economy of the New Left: An Outsider's View*. New York: Harper and Row, 1977.

Lindqvist, Martti. *Economic Growth and the Quality of Life*. Helsinki: Finnish Society for Missiology and Ecumenics, 1975.

Lissner, Jorgen. *The Politics of Altruism: A Study of the Behavior of Voluntary Development Agencies*. Geneva: Lutheran World Federation, 1977.

Luther, Martin. "The Small Catechism." *The Book of Concord*. Edited and translated by Theodore G. Tappert. Philadelphia: Fortress Press, 1959.

Lutheran Book of Worship. Prepared by the churches participating in the Inter-Lutheran Commission on Worship. Minneapolis/ Philadelphia: Augsburg Publishing House/Board of Publication, LCA, 1978.

MacPherson, C.B. *The Political Theory of Possessive Individualism: Hobbes to Locke*. Cambridge: Oxford University Press, 1962.

McGinnis, James B. *Bread and Justice: Toward a New International Order*. New York: Paulist Press, 1979.

Minutes. Ninth Biennial Convention of the Lutheran Church in America, July 12-19, 1978.

Minutes. Seventh Biennial Convention of the Lutheran Church in America, July 3-10, 1974.

Moeller, Bernard. *Imperial Cities and the Reformation*. Edited and translated by Eric H.C. Midelfort and Mark U. Edwards Jr. Philadelphia: Fortress Press, 1972.

Moses, Stanley. "Planning for Full Employment." In *Annals of the American Academy of Political and Social Science*. Philadelphia, 1975.

Munby, D.L. *Christianity and Economic Problems*. London: Macmillan, 1956.

Myrdal, Gunnar. *Against the Stream: Critical Essays on Economics*. New York: Vintage Books, 1972.

Niebuhr, Reinhold. *Moral Man and Immoral Society*. New York: Charles Scribner's Sons, 1932.

Norman, Edward. *Church and Society in England, 1170-1970: A Historical Study*. Oxford: Clarendon Press, 1976.

Raschke, Carl A. *The Bursting of New Wineskins: Reflections on Religion and Culture at the End of Affluence*. New York: Pickwick Press, 1978.

Rasmussen, Larry, and Birch, Bruce. *The Predicament of the Prosperous*. Philadelphia: Westminster Press, 1979.

Rawls, John. *A Theory of Justice*. Cambridge, Massachusetts: Belknap Press of Harvard University Press, 1971.

Richards, Howard. "Adam Smith, Milton Friedman and Christian Economics," *The Earth is the Lord's*. Edited by Mary Evelyn Jegan and Bruno V. Manno. New York: Paulist Press, 1978.

Rifkin, Jeremy, and Barber, Randy. *The North Will Rise Again: Pensions, Politics and Power in the 1980's*. Boston: Beacon Press, 1978.

Rockefeller Foundation. *The Search for a Value Consensus*. New York: Rockefeller Foundation, 1978.

Rusow, Jerome M. *The Worker and the Job*. New York: Columbia University Press, 1974.

Said, Abdul Aziz, ed. *Human Rights and World Order*. New York: Praeger, 1978.

Schrank, Robert. *Ten Thousand Working Days*. Cambridge, Massachusetts: MIT Press, 1978.

Schultz, Theodore N. *Investment in Human Capital*. New York: Free Press, 1970.

Segundo, S.J., Juan Luis. *The Liberation of Theology*. Maryknoll, New York: Orbis Books, 1976.

Seidman, Ann, and Seidman, Neva. *South Africa and U.S. Multinational Corporations*. Westport, Connecticut: Hill, 1977.

Shepherd, Harold L., and Rix, Sara E. *The Graying of Working America: The Coming Crisis of Retirement Age Policy*. New York: Free Press, 1977.

Shoemaker, E.F. *Small is Beautiful*. New York: Harper and Row, 1973.

Smith, Adam. *The Theory of Moral Sentiments*. London: Henry C. Bohn, 1961.

Smith, Adam. *The Wealth of Nations*. New York: Random House, 1957.

Social Statements, 1964-1980. The Lutheran Church in America, 231 Madison Avenue, New York, New York.

Tappert, Theodore G., ed. *The Book of Concord*. Philadelphia: Fortress Press, 1959.

"The No-Growth Society." *Daedalus: Journal of the American Academy of Arts and Sciences,* Fall 1973.

Thielicke, Helmut. *Theological Ethics*. Translated by William H. Lazareth. Philadelphia: Fortress Press, 1960.

Tillich, Paul. *The Socialist Decision*. Translated by Franklin Sherman. New York: Harper and Row, 1977.

Ting, K.H. (Ding Kuangumn). "A Sermon by K.H. Ting." *Information Letter: Marxism and China Study*. Geneva: Lutheran World Federation, October 1979, p. 18.

Tumsa, Gudina. "The Role of a Christian in a Given Society." *Lutheran World Information,* 13 February 1980, p. 18.

Updike, John. *The Coup*. New York: Fawcett Crest, 1978.

United Nations Centre for Disarmament. *Economic and Social Consequences of the Arms Race and of Military Expenditures*. Updated Report of the Secretary-General. United Nations, 1978.

Vickrey, William. "An Economist's View of Human Rights." *Small Comfort in Hard Times*. Edited by Michael Mooney and Florian Stuber. New York: Columbia University Press, 1977.

Vickrey, William. "An Exchange of Questions Between Economics and Philosophy." *Goals of Economic Life*. Edited by A.D. Ward. New York: Harper, 1953, p. 56.